Dedication

For Jared, כי אהבת נפשי, אהבו

Contents
at a Glance

Contents

Foreword

By Dave Winer, CEO, UserLand Software

I remember as if it were yesterday my first experience with a user. I had been developing a software product for three years, all the while thinking it was easy to use. A friend who had been listening to me gush about how great it was asked if he could try it. Hesitantly, I said yes. I launched the program and we switched seats. I tried to say nothing as he wondered what to do. The software didn't have anything to say. "What should I do?" he asked. I thought to myself, "I have some work to do."

This is the moment of truth for any software developer, and one we avoid. In *The Soul of a New Machine*, Tracy Kidder tells about the first problem report from "the field" about a computer system developed at Data General in the late 1970s. The lead developer was surprised. In his mind the computer was a development project; that real people would try to *use* it attacked his perception of his own product.

We all go through this; at a superficial level we think we're designing for users, but no matter how hard we try, we're designing for who we think the user is, and that means, sadly, that we're designing for ourselves. Until you prove that it's usable by other people, your software is certainly *not* designed for them.

Until you make the shift and let the users tell you how your software works, it simply can't be usable. Every successful software product is proof of this, as is every failure. How many times have you installed some software or visited a Web site and wondered, "What does this do?" Now, understand that other people are asking the same question about your software. It's a puzzle, to solve it you must figure out how to get your software into a user's mind, and to learn how to do that, you must learn how that mind works.

Joel's book is a milestone built on a strong foundation of practical experience. He's absolutely right that user testing is easy. You don't need a lab to do it, although many people think you do. You just need a computer and a person who doesn't know your software. It's an iterative process. Do it once, it'll change your whole perspective. Do some engineering. Do it again with a new person. Repeat the process until the first-time user knows what to do and can actually use the software to do what it was designed to do.

Joel's book is about more than software design and user-centricity. Once you learn how to communicate with users through software, it's inevitable that all your communication will improve. The central "aha" is to realize that other people use your software, and they don't know what you know, and they don't think like you think they do.

There are some very simple truths in this book, and sometimes the simplest truths can be most difficult. But Joel makes it so easy! His stories are clear and human and fun. And that may be the biggest lesson, if you haven't been designing for users, you're not having as much fun doing software as you could.

I can tell you from personal experience that there's nothing more satisfying as a professional software developer than to have a product resonate with the market, to have thousands of people tell you that they couldn't work without your software. To get there, you have to learn from them as you teach. Yes, your software is great, I believe you, but if no one uses it, it can't make the world a better place.

Dave Winer
http://www.scripting.com/

Introduction

Most of the hard core C++ programmers I know *hate* user interface programming. This surprises me because I find UI programming to be quintessentially easy, straightforward, and fun.

It's *easy* because you usually don't need algorithms more sophisticated than how to center one rectangle in another. It's *straightforward* because when you make a mistake, you can see it right away and correct it. It's *fun* because the results of your work are immediately visible. You feel like you are sculpting the program directly.

I think most programmers' fear of UI programming comes from their fear of doing UI *design*. They think that UI design is like graphic design: that mysterious process by which creative, latte-drinking, all-dressed-in-black people with interesting piercings produce cool-looking artistic stuff. Programmers see themselves as analytic, logical thinkers: strong at reasoning, weak on artistic judgment. So they think they can't do UI design.

Actually, I've found UI design to be quite easy and quite rational. It's not a mysterious matter that requires an art school degree and a penchant for neon-purple hair. There is a rational way to think about user interfaces with some simple, logical rules that you can apply anywhere to improve the interfaces of the programs you work on.

This book is not *Zen and the Art of UI Design*. It's not art, it's not Buddhism, it's just a set of rules. A way of thinking rationally and methodically. This book is designed for programmers. I assume you don't need instructions for *how* to make a menu bar; rather, you need to think about what to put in your menu bar (or whether to have one at all). You'll learn the primary axiom which guides all good UI design and some of the corollaries. We'll look at some examples from real life, modern GUI programs. When you're done, you'll know enough to be a significantly better UI designer.

Acknowledgments

I would like to thank Gary Cornell at Apress for making this book possible and Allen Holub for reviewing it. Without the encouragement of Noah Tratt, I never would have started writing down my experiences in the software trenches, and without the support of Dave Winer and his public EditThisPage.com system, I wouldn't have had a forum for writing the original online version of this book. Many thanks also to the hundreds of readers of Joel on Software (http://joel.editthispage.com) who responded to the original articles, proposed numerous corrections and enhancements, and whose frequent fan mail kept me going. I also want to thank Andrew Kwatinetz at Microsoft who taught me a lot of what I know about UI design; Ken Dye, who taught me most of what I know about usability testing; and Joseph Roberts, who taught me all the tricks of localization. I am also grateful to Jared Samet for proof-reading the final document, encouraging me, and believing in me, and my parents, who made me grow up thinking that *all* adults write books.

1

Controlling Your Environment Makes You Happy

My first real job was in a big industrial bakery that churned out hundreds of thousands of loaves of bread every night. The bakery was designed to have six bread production lines. For every two production lines, there was a dough mixer, which produced these gigantic 180 kg lumps of dough that could be dumped to the left or the right, as shown in Figure 1-1.

FIGURE 1-1

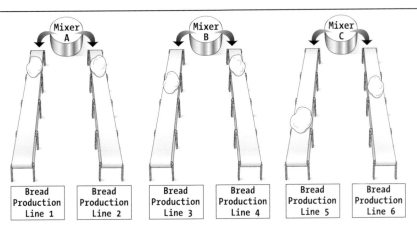

The bakery, as designed

Well, this was the design. In reality, Mixer C hadn't been built yet, nor had lines three or five. So the arrangement was more like Figure 1-2.

FIGURE 1-2

The bakery, as implemented

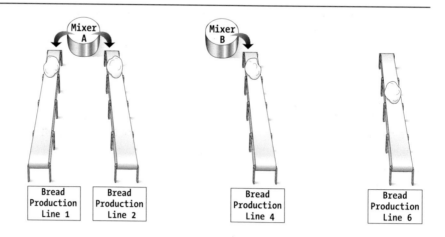

Alert readers will be wondering, "how did the dough get from Mixer B to production line six?" Well, that's where Wee Joel came in. My job, if you can believe this, was to stand to the left of Mixer B, then *catch* these walrus-sized lumps of dough as they flew out of the mixer in a big bathtub with wheels, then roll the bathtub over to production line six, and using a winchlike device, heave the dough onto the line. I had to do this once every ten minutes from about 10 P.M. until 4 A.M.

There were other complications. Line six couldn't really handle 180 kg of dough all at once, so I had to slice each blob with a giant knife into about ten pieces. I don't even want to go into how absurdly difficult *that* was.

The first few days, of course, I was terrible at this job. It seemed nearly impossible. Every bone in my body ached. My blisters had blisters. I had aches in places where I didn't know I had places.

At first I just couldn't keep line six supplied with dough. Every time I got behind in supplying the dough, there was a big gap on the assembly line. When the gap rolled into the oven, the oven (expending a constant amount of energy over a reduced amount of dough) started to heat up more, which burnt the bread.

Sometimes line six would get gummed up and stop running, but the mixer went right on ahead producing dough for me and I ran the risk of running out of enough bathtubs-with-wheels to store the dough in. When this happened, I had to clean and oil the floor and actually dump the dough onto the floor to be scraped up later. Not that this worked very well, because if the dough got older than about thirty minutes it would ferment into unintentional sourdough. If this happened, you had to chop it up into five kg pieces and put one piece into the mixture for each future batch.

After a week or so, I became good enough at the routine that I actually had, if I remember correctly, two minutes free for every ten-minute dough-cycle to rest. I figured out a precise schedule and learned how to tell the mixer to skip a batch when the production line stopped.

And I started to think about why, as the beer commercial asks, *some days are better than others.*

One day, thinking about this problem, I noticed that one of the bathtubs-with-wheels had pretty lousy wheels that wouldn't turn well. Sometimes this bathtub did not go where I pushed it, and bumped into things. This was a small frustration. Sometimes, as I was pulling the chain to winch up the bathtub, I scraped myself—just a little bit—on a splinter of metal on the chain. Another small frustration. Sometimes, as I ran with an empty bathtub to catch a dough emission about to fly out of the mixer, I slipped on a little bit of oil on the floor. Not enough to fall, mind you, just a tiny slip producing a tiny frustration.

Other times, I would have tiny victories. I learned to time the dough production perfectly so that fresh dough would arrive just *seconds* before the previous batch ran out. This guaranteed the freshest dough and made the best bread. Some of the victories were even tinier: I would spot a strawberry-sized blob of dough that had flung off of the mixer and attached itself to the wall, and I would scrape it off with a paint scraper I carried in my back pocket and throw it in the trash. *Yes!* When slicing the dough into pieces, sometimes it just sliced really *nicely* and *easily*. These were tiny moments of satisfaction when I managed to control the world around me, even in the smallest way.

So that's what days were like. A bunch of tiny frustrations, and a bunch of tiny successes. But they *added up.* Even something that seems like a tiny, inconsequential frustration affects your mood. Your emotions don't seem to care about the magnitude of the event, only the quality.

And I started to learn that the days when I was happiest were the days with a lot of small successes and few small frustrations.

Years later, when I got to college, I learned about an important theory of psychology called Learned Helplessness, developed by Dr. Martin E. P. Seligman. This theory, backed up by years of research, is that a great deal of depression grows out of a feeling of *helplessness*: the feeling that you cannot control your environment.

The more you feel that you can control your environment, and that the things you do are actually working, the happier you are.

When you find yourself frustrated, angry, and upset, it's probably because something happened that you could not control: even something small. The space bar on your keyboard is not working well. When you type, some of the words are stuck together. This gets frustrating, because you are pressing the space bar and *nothing is happening*. The key to your front door doesn't work very well. When you try to turn it, it sticks. Another tiny frustration. These things add up; these are the situations that make us unhappy on a day-to-day basis. Even though they seem too petty to dwell on (I mean, there are people *starving* in Africa, for heaven's sake, I can't get upset about *space bars*), nonetheless, they change our moods.

Let's pause for a minute and go back to computers.

We're going to invent a typical Windows power user named Pete. When you're thinking about user interfaces, it helps to keep imaginary users in mind. The more realistic the imaginary user is, the better you'll do in thinking about how they use your product.

Pete is an accountant for a technical publisher who has used Windows for six years at the office and a bit at home. He is fairly competent and technical. He installs his own software; he reads PC Magazine; and he has even programmed some simple Word macros to help the secretaries in his office send invoices. He's getting a cable modem at home. Pete has never used a Macintosh. "They're too expensive," he'll tell you. "You can get a 733 MHz PC with 128 Meg RAM for the price of..." OK, Pete. We get it.

One day, Pete's friend Gena asks him for some computer help. Now, Gena has a Macintosh iBook because she loves the translucent boxes. When Pete sits down and tries to use the Macintosh, he quickly becomes frustrated. "I hate these things," he says. He is finally able to help Gena, but he's grumpy and unhappy. "The Macintosh has such a clunky user interface."

Clunky? What's he talking about? *Everybody* knows that the Macintosh has an elegant user interface, right? The very *paradigm* of ease-of-use?

Here's my analysis of this mystery.

On the Macintosh, when you want to move a window, you can grab any edge with the mouse and move it. On Windows, you must grab the title bar. If you try to grab an edge, the window will be reshaped. When Pete was helping Gena, he tried to widen a window by dragging the right edge. Frustratingly, the whole window moved rather than resizing as he expected.

On Windows, when a message box pops up, you can hit Enter *or* the space bar to dismiss the message box. On the Mac, space doesn't work. You usually need to click with the mouse. When Pete got alerts, he tried to dismiss them using the space bar like he's been doing subconsciously for the last six years. The first time, nothing happened. Without even being aware of it, Pete banged the space bar harder since he thought that the problem must be that the Mac did not register his tapping the space bar. Actually, it did—but it didn't care! Eventually he used the mouse. Another tiny frustration.

Pete has also learned to use Alt+F4 to close windows. On the Mac, this actually changes the *volume of the speakers*. At one point, Pete wanted to click on the Internet Explorer icon on the desktop, which was partially covered by another window. So he hit Alt+F4 to close the window and immediately double-clicked where the icon would have been. The Alt+F4 raised the volume on the computer and didn't close the window, so his double click actually went to the Help button in the toolbar on the window (which he wanted closed *anyway*), and that started bringing up a help window, painfully slowly, so now he's got *two* windows open that he has to close. Another small frustration, but, boy, does it add up.

At the end of the day, Pete is grumpy and angry. When he tries to control things, they don't respond. The space bar and the Alt+F4 key "don't work"—for all intents and purposes it's as if those keys were broken. The window disobeys when he tries to make it wider by playing a little prank: it just moves over instead of widening. Bad window. Even if the whole thing is subconscious, the subtle feeling of being out of control translates into helplessness, which translates into unhappiness. "I like my computer," Pete says. "I have it all set up so that it works exactly the way I like it. But these Macs are clunky and hard to use. It's an exercise in frustration. If Apple had been working on MacOS all these years instead of messing around with Newtons, their operating system wouldn't be such a mess."

Right, Pete. We know better. His feelings come *despite* the fact that the Macintosh really is quite easy to use—for Mac users. To close a window, it's totally arbitrary which key you press. The Microsoft programmers who were, presumably, copying the Mac interface probably thought that they were adding a cool new feature in letting you resize

windows by dragging any edge. And the MacOS 8 programmers probably thought that they were adding a cool new feature when they let
you move windows by dragging any edge.

Most flame wars you read about user interface issues focus on the
wrong thing. Windows is better because it gives you *more ways* to resize
the window. So what? That's missing the point. The point is, does the
UI respond to the user in the way in which the user *expected* it to
respond? If it didn't, the user is going to feel helpless and out of control,
the same way I felt when the wheels of the dough-bathtub didn't turn
the way I pushed them, and I bumped into a wall. Bonk.

UI is important because it affects the feelings, the emotions, and
the mood of your users. If the UI is wrong and the user feels like they
can't control your software, they *literally* won't be happy and they'll
blame it on your software. If the UI is smart and things work the way the
user expected them to work, they will be cheerful as they manage to
accomplish small goals. Hey! I ripped a CD! It *just worked! Nice software!!*

To make people happy, you have to let them feel like they are in
control of their environment. To do this, you need to *correctly* interpret
their actions. The interface needs to behave in the way they expect it
to behave.

Thus, the cardinal axiom of all user interface design:

> *A user interface is well designed when*
> *the program behaves exactly how the user*
> *thought it would.*

As Hillel said, everything else is commentary. All the other rules
of good UI design are just corollaries.

2

Figuring Out What They Expected

When I was in college many years ago, a friend of mine down the hall pulled an all-nighter. A critical term paper was due the next day, and he stayed up until 6 A.M. banging away on his Macintosh. Finally, bleary-eyed, he turned off the computer and tried to catch a couple of hours of sleep before the paper was due.

Yep.

He turned off the computer.

Notice I didn't say that he saved his work and turned off the computer. At 6 A.M., he forgot about that little thing.

At about 7:45 A.M., he came knocking on my dorm room door in despair. "Um, you know computers," he was practically crying. "Can't I get my paper back?"

"You didn't save it *at all*?" I asked.

"Nope."

"Never? All night long you never *once* hit 'Save?'"

"No. It was still called 'Untitled.' But it's in there *somewhere*, isn't it?"

The Macintosh in its WYSIWYG glory simulates the act of typing on a piece of paper so perfectly that nothing interfered with my friend's sad idea that his paper was in there, *somewhere*. When you write on a piece of paper, that's it! Done! The paper is now *written*. There's no *Save* operation for paper.

A new user who sits down to use a program does not come with a completely blank slate. They have some expectations of how they think the program is going to work. This is called the *user model*: it is their mental understanding of what the program will do for them.

If they've never used a computer before, and the computer shows them what looks like a piece of paper and lets them type on it, then they are completely justified in assuming that they won't need to save their work.

Experienced users have user models, too: if they've used similar software before, they will assume it's going to work like that other software. If you've used WordPerfect but not Word, when you sit down to use Word, you assume that you must save.

The program, too, has a model, only this one is encoded in bits and will be faithfully executed by the CPU. This is called the *program model*, and it is *The Law*. Nothing short of electrical storms and cosmic rays can convince a CPU to disobey the program model.

Now, remember the cardinal axiom from Chapter 1? You should have memorized it by now:

> *A user interface is well designed when the program behaves exactly how the user thought it would.*

Another way of saying this is:

> *A user interface is well designed when the program model conforms to the user model.*

That's it. Almost all good user interface design comes down to bringing the program model and the user model in line. The Macintosh UI would have been more successful (especially for my poor friend) if it saved your "unsaved" work for you. Of course, in 1985, the slow speed of floppy disks made this impractical. But in 1988, by which time everybody had hard drives, this became inexcusable. To this day, most popular software doesn't automatically save your work.

Let's look at another example. In Microsoft Word (and most word processors), when you put a picture in your document, the picture is actually embedded in the same file as the document itself. You can create the picture, drag it into the document, then *delete the original picture file*, but the picture will still remain in the document.

Now, HTML doesn't let you do this. HTML documents must store their pictures in a separate file. If you take a user who is used to word processors and doesn't know anything about HTML, then sit them down in front of a nice WYSIWYG HTML editor like Microsoft FrontPage, they will almost certainly think that the picture is going to be stored in the file. Call this *user model inertia*, if you will.

So, we have an unhappy conflict of user model (the picture will be embedded) versus program model (the picture must be in a separate file), and the UI is bound to cause problems.

If you're designing a program like FrontPage, you've just found your first UI problem. You can't really change HTML; after all, it's an international standard. Something has to give to bring the program model in line with the user model.

You have a couple of choices. You can try to change the user model. This turns out to be remarkably hard. You could explain things in the manual, but everybody knows that users don't read manuals, and they probably shouldn't have to. Or, you can pop up a little dialog box explaining that the image file won't be embedded—but this has *two* problems: it's annoying to sophisticated users; and users don't read dialog boxes, either. We'll talk more about this in Chapter 9.

So, if the mountain won't come to Muhammad, Muhammad must go to the mountain. Your best choice is almost always going to be to change the program model, not the user model. Perhaps when the user inserts picture, the program should make a copy of the picture in a subdirectory beneath the document file—this, at least, conforms to the user's idea that the picture is copied (and the original can safely be deleted).

How Do I Know What the User Model Is?

This turns out to be relatively easy. Just ask some users! Pick five random people in your office, or friends, or family, and tell them what your program does in general terms ("it's a program for making Web pages"). Then describe the situation: "You've got a Web page that you're working on and a picture file named Picture.JPG. You insert the picture into your Web page." Then ask them some questions to try and guess their user model. "Where did the picture go? If you delete the Picture.JPG file, will the Web page still be able to show the picture?"

A friend of mine is working on a photo album application. After you insert your photos, the application shows you a bunch of thumbnails: wee copies of each picture. Now, generating these thumbnails takes a long time, especially if you have a lot of pictures, so he wants to store the thumbnails on the hard drive *somewhere* so that they only have to be generated once. There are a lot of ways he could do this. They could all be stored in one large file called `Thumbnails` in some-place annoying like `C:\`. They could all be stored in separate files in a subdirectory called `Thumbnails`. They might be marked as hidden files in the operating system so that users don't know about them. My friend chose one way of doing it that he thought was the best tradeoff: he stored the thumbnail of each picture, `picture.JPG`, in a new file named `picture_t.JPG` within the same directory. If you made an album with thirty pictures, when you were finished, there would be *sixty* files in the directory including the thumbnails!

You could argue for weeks about the merits and demerits of various picture-storing schemes, but as it turns out, there's a more scientific way to do it. Just ask a bunch of users where they think the thumb-nails are going to be stored. Of course, many of them won't know or won't care, or they won't have thought about this. But if you ask a lot of people, you'll start to see *some* kind of consensus. As it turns out, not very many people expected the `picture_t.JPG` file, so he changed the program to create a `Thumbnails` subdirectory.

The popular choice is the best user model, and it's up to you to make the program model match it.

The next step is to test your theories. Build a model or prototype of your user interface and give some people tasks to accomplish. The model can be extremely simple: sometimes it's enough to draw a sloppy picture of the user interface on a piece of paper and walk around the office asking people how they would accomplish *x* with the "program" you drew.

As they work through the tasks, ask them what they think is hap-pening. Your goal is to figure out what they expect. If the task is to "insert a picture," and you see that they are trying to drag the picture into your program, you'll realize that you had better support drag and drop. If they go to the Insert menu, you'll realize that you had better have a Picture choice in the Insert menu. If they go to the Font toolbar and replace the word "Times New Roman" with the words "Insert Picture", you've found one of those old relics who hasn't been intro-duced to GUIs yet and is expecting a command-line interface.

How many users do you need to test your interface on? The scien-tific approach seems like it would be "the more, the better." If testing on five users is good, testing on twenty users is *better*!

But that approach is flat-out wrong. Almost everybody who does usability testing for a living agrees that five or six users is all you need. After that, you start seeing the same results again and again, and any additional users are just a waste of time. The reason being that you don't particularly care about the exact numerical statistics of failure. You simply want to discover what "most people" think.

You don't need a formal usability lab, and you don't really need to bring in users "off the street"—you can do "fifty-cent usability tests" where you simply grab the next person you see and ask them to try a quick usability test. Make sure you don't spill the beans and tell them how to do things. Ask them to think out loud and interview them using open questions to try to discover their mental model.

If Your Program Model Is Nontrivial, It's Probably Not the Same As the User Model

When I was six and my dad brought home one of the world's first pocket calculators, an HP-35, he tried to convince me that it had a *computer* inside it. I thought that was unlikely. All the computers on Star Trek were the size of a room and had big reel-to-reel tape recorders. I tried to convince my dad that the calculator worked simply by having a straightforward correlation between the keys on the keypad and the individual elements of the LED display, which happened to produce mathematically correct results. (Hey, I was *six*.)

An important rule of thumb is that user models aren't very complex. When people have to guess how a program is going to work, they tend to guess simple things rather than complicated things.

Sit down at a Macintosh. Open two Excel spreadsheet files and one Word document file, as shown in Figure 2-1.

Almost any novice user would guess that the windows are independent. They *look* independent.

The user model says that clicking on Spreadsheet 1 will bring that window to the front. What *really* happens is that *Spreadsheet 2* comes to the front, as shown in Figure 2-2, a frustrating surprise for almost anybody.

As it turns out, Microsoft Excel's program model says, "you have these invisible sheets, like cellophane, one for each application. The windows are 'glued' to those invisible sheets. When you bring Excel to the foreground, you are really clicking on the cellophane, so all the other windows from Excel should move forward too without changing their order."

Riiiiiiiiight. Invisible sheets. What are the chances that the user model included the concept of invisible sheets? Probably zero. The user model is a lot simpler: "The windows are like pieces of paper on a desk." End of story. So new users are inevitably surprised by Excel's behavior.

FIGURE 2-1

Guess what happens when you click on Spreadsheet 1?

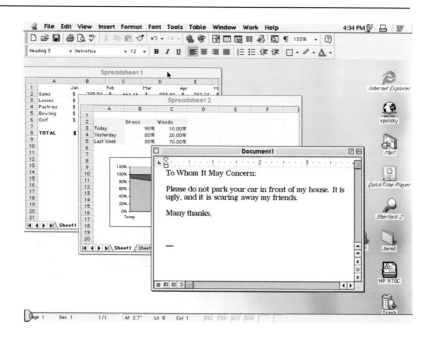

FIGURE 2-2

Wrong! Microsoft Excel's program model includes the bizarre and unlikely concept of an invisible sheet that all the other sheets are glued onto.

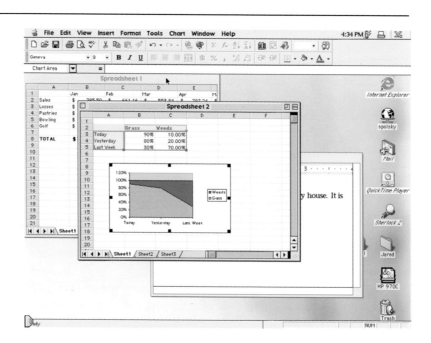

Another example from the world of Microsoft Windows concerns the Alt+Tab key combination, which switches to the "next" window. Most users would probably assume that it simply rotates among all available windows. If you have windows A, B, and C, with A active, Alt+Tab should take you to B. Pressing Alt+Tab again would take you to C. Actually, what happens is that the second Alt+Tab takes you back to A. The only way to get to C is to *hold down* Alt and press Tab *twice*. It's a nice way to toggle between two applications, but almost nobody figures it out because it's a slightly more complicated model than the rotate-among-available-windows model.

Users will assume
the simplest model possible.

It's hard enough to make the program model conform to the user model when the models are simple. When the models become complex, it's even more unlikely. So pick the simplest model possible.

3

Choices

When you go into a restaurant and see a sign that says "No Dogs Allowed," you might think that sign is purely proscriptive: Mr. Restaurant doesn't like dogs around, so when he built the restaurant he put up that sign.

If that was *all* that was going on, there would also be a "No Snakes" sign; after all, nobody likes snakes. And a "No Elephants" sign, because they break the chairs when they sit down.

The *real* reason that sign is there is historical: it is a historical marker that indicates that people used to try to bring their dogs into the restaurant.

Most prohibitive signs are there because the proprietors of an establishment were sick and tired of people doing *x*, so they made a sign asking them to please *not*. If you go into one of those fifty-year-old Ma-and-Pa diners like the Yankee Doodle in New Haven, the walls are *covered* with signs saying things like "Please don't put your knapsack on the counter"—more anthropological evidence that people used to put their knapsacks on the counter a lot. By the yellowing of the sign, you can figure out when knapsacks were popular among local students.

Sometimes it's a bit tricky to figure out the history behind the sign. "Please do not bring glass bottles into the park" must mean that somebody cut themselves stepping on broken glass while walking barefoot through the grass once. It's a good bet they sued the city, and now the city puts up signs.

FIGURE 3-1

Most signs, especially handwritten ones, are historical records.

Legal contracts contain archaeological artifacts, too. The reason legal agreements are so dang complicated and say dumb things like "worker, laborer, operative, roustabout, workhand, workingman, workman, artisan, craftsman, handicraftsman, mechanic, or employee" instead of just "worker" is because there was probably some lawsuit in 1873 where someone got out of a contract because he successfully argued in court that he was a roustabout, not a worker.

Software has a similar archaeological record, too: it's called the Options dialog. Pull up the Tools ➤ Options dialog box and you will see a history of the heated arguments that the software designers had about the design of the product. Should we automatically open the last file that the user was working on? Yes! No! There is a two-week debate, nobody wants to hurt anyone's feelings, the programmer puts in an `#ifdef` in self-defense while the designers fight it out. Eventually they just decide to make it an option. One more thing in Tools ➤ Options can't hurt, can it?

It doesn't even have to be a debate between two people: it can be an internal dilemma. "I just *can't decide* if we should optimize the database for size or optimize for speed." Either way, you wind up with things like what is unequivocally the most moronic "wizard" dialog in the history of the Windows operating system. This dialog is so stupid

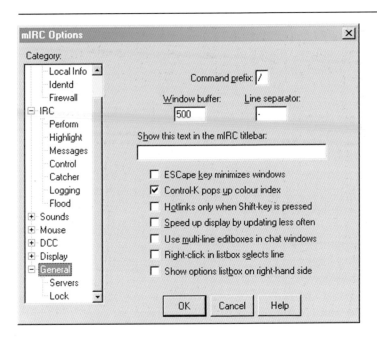

FIGURE 3-2

Options dialogs often become nothing more than a journal of the designer's indecision.

that it deserves some kind of award. A whole new *category* of award. It's the dialog that comes up when you try to find something in Help, as shown in Figure 3-3.

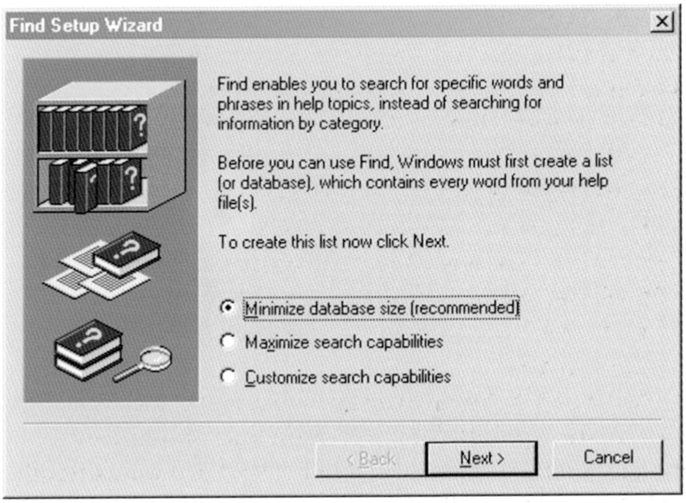

FIGURE 3-3

The most moronic wizard dialog Microsoft has ever shipped

The first problem with this dialog is that it's distracting. You are trying to find help in the help file. You do not, at that particular moment, give a *hoot* whether the database is small, big, customized, or chocolate-covered. In the meanwhile, this wicked, wicked dialog is giving you pedantic little lectures that it must create a list (or database). There are about three paragraphs there, most of which are completely confusing. There's the painfully awkward phrase "your help file(s)". You see, you may have *one or more* files. As if you *cared* at this point that there could be more than one. As if it made the slightest amount of difference. But the programmer who worked on that dialog was obviously distressed beyond belief at the possibility that there might be more than one help file(s) and it would be incorrect to say help file, now, wouldn't it?

Don't even get me started about how most people who want help are not the kinds of people who understand these kinds of arcana. Or that even advanced users, programmers with Ph.D.s in Computer Science who know *all about* full text indexes, would not be able to figure out just what the heck they are really being asked to choose from.

To add insult to injury, this isn't even a dialog... it's a *wizard* (the second page of which just says something like "thank you for submitting yourself to this needless waste of your time," to paraphrase). And it's pretty obvious that the designers had *some* idea as to which choice is best; after all, they've gone to the trouble of recommending one of the choices.

Which brings us to our second major rule of user interface design:

> *Every time you provide an option, you're*
>
> *asking the user to make a decision.*

Asking the user to make a decision isn't *in itself* a bad thing. Freedom of choice can be wonderful. People *love* to order espresso-based beverages at Starbucks because they get to make so many *choices*. Grande, half-caf, skim Mocha Valencia with whip. Extra hot!

The problem comes when you ask them to make a choice that *they don't care about*. In the case of help files, people are looking at the help file because they are having trouble accomplishing something they *really want to accomplish*, like making a birthday invitation. Their birthday invitation task has been unfortunately interrupted because they can't figure out how to print upside-down balloons, or whatever, so they go to the help file. Now, some annoying help-index-engine-programmer at Microsoft with an inflated idea of his own importance in the whole scheme of things has the *audacity*, the *chutzpah*, to interrupt this user *once again* and start teaching them things about making lists (or databases). This second level of interrupting is completely unrelated to birthday invitations, and it's simply guaranteed to perplex and eventually piss off the user.

And believe you me, users care about a lot fewer things than you might think. They are using your software to accomplish a task. They care about the task. If it's a graphics program, they probably want to be able to control *every pixel* to the finest level of detail. If it's a tool to build a Web site, you can bet that they are obsessive about getting the Web site to look exactly the way they want it to look.

They do *not*, however, care one whit if the program's own toolbar is on the top or the bottom of the window. They don't care how the help file is indexed. They don't care about a lot of things, and it is the designers' responsibility to make these choices for them so that they don't have to. It is the height of arrogance for a software designer to inflict a choice like this on the user simply because the designer couldn't think hard enough to decide which option is really better. (It's even worse when you try to cover up the fact that you're giving the user a difficult choice by converting it to a wizard, as the WinHelp people did. As if the user is a moron who needs to take a little two-step mini-course in the choice they are being offered so that they can make an *educated* decision.)

It has been said that design is the art of *making choices*. When you design a trash can for the corner, you have to make choices between conflicting requirements. It needs to be heavy so it won't blow away. It needs to be light so the trash collector can dump it out. It needs to be large so it can hold a lot of trash. It needs to be small so it doesn't get in peoples' way on the sidewalk. It needs to be open so people can throw trash in it. It needs to be closed so trash doesn't blow out on windy days.

When you are designing and you try to abdicate your responsibility by forcing the user to decide something, you're not doing your job. Someone else will make an easier program that accomplishes the same task with fewer intrusions, and most users will love it.

When Microsoft Excel 3.0 came out in 1990, it was the first Windows application to sport a new feature called a toolbar. It was a sensible feature, people liked it, and everybody copied it—to the point that it's unusual to see an application without one any more.

The toolbar was so successful that the Excel team did field research using a special version of the software which they distributed to a few friends; this version kept statistics on what the most frequently used commands were and reported them back to Microsoft. For the next version, they added a *second* row of toolbar buttons, this time containing the most frequently used commands. Great.

The trouble was, they never got around to disbanding the toolbar team, who didn't seem to know when to leave good enough alone. They wanted you to be able to *customize* your toolbar. They wanted you to be able to drag the toolbar anywhere on the screen. Then, they started to think about how the menu bar is really just a glorified toolbar with words instead of icons, so they let you drag the *menu bar* anywhere you wanted on the screen, too. Customizability on steroids. Problem: nobody cares! I've never met anyone who wants their menu bar anywhere except at the top of the window. But here's the (bad) joke: if you try to pull down the File menu and accidentally grab the menu bar a tiny bit too far to the left, you yank off the whole menu bar, dragging it to the only place you could not possibly want it to be: blocking the document you're working on as shown in Figure 3-4.

FIGURE 3-4

Miss the File menu by a couple of pixels and the whole menu bar comes flying off.

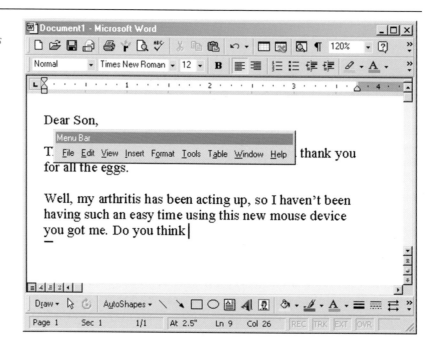

How many times have you seen *that*? And once you've done this by mistake, it's not clear what you did or how to fix it. So, here we have an option (moving the menu bar) that nobody wants (ok, maybe 0.1% of all humans want it) but which gets in the way for almost everybody.

One day a friend called me up. She was having trouble sending email. "Half the screen is grey," she said.

Half the screen is grey?

It took me five minutes over the phone to figure out what had happened. She had accidentally dragged the Windows toolbar to the right side of the screen, then accidentally widened it as shown in Figure 3-5.

FIGURE 3-5

Half the screen is grey.

This is the kind of thing that nobody does *on purpose*. And there are a lot of computer users out there who can't get themselves out of this kind of mess. Almost by *definition*, when you accidentally reconfigure one of the options in your program, you don't know how to re-reconfigure it. It's sort of shocking to see how many people uninstall and then reinstall their software when things start behaving wrong, because at least they know how to do that. (They've learned to uninstall first, because otherwise all the broken customizations are likely to just come back).

"But wait!" you say. "It's important to have options for *advanced* users who want to tweak their environments!" In reality, it's not as important as you think. This reminds me of when I tried to switch to a Dvorak keyboard. The trouble was, I don't use *one* computer. I use all kinds of computers. I use other people's computers. I use three computers fairly regularly at home and three at work. I use computers in the test lab at work. The trouble with customizing your environment is that it just doesn't *propagate*, so it's not even worth the trouble.

Most advanced users use several computers regularly; they upgrade their computer every couple of years, and they reinstall their operating system every three weeks. It's true that the *first* time they realized they could completely remap the keyboard in Word, they might have changed everything around to be more to their taste. But as soon as they upgraded to Windows 95, those settings were lost. Besides, they weren't the same at work. So eventually they just stopped reconfiguring things. I've asked a lot of my power user friends about this; hardly any of them do any customization other than the bare minimum necessary to make their system behave reasonably.

Every time you provide an option, you're asking the user to make a decision. This means that they will have to stop and think. That's not necessarily a *bad* thing, but in general, you should always try to minimize the number of decisions that people have to make.

This doesn't mean eliminate *all* choice. There are enough choices that users will have to make anyway: the way their document will look, the way their Web site will behave, or anything else that is integral to the work that the user is doing. In these areas, go crazy: it's great to give people choices; by all means, the more the merrier.

There's another category of choice that people seem to like: the ability to change the visual look of things without really changing the behavior. Everybody loves WinAmp skins; everybody sets their desktop background to a picture. Since the choice affects the visual look without affecting the way anything functions, and since users are completely free to ignore the choice and get their work done anyway, this is a good use of options.

4

Affordances and Metaphors

Developing a user interface where the program model matches the user model is not easy. Sometimes, your users might not have a concrete expectation of how the program works and what it's supposed to do. There is no user model.

When the user model is incomplete or wrong, the program can use affordances or metaphors to show the user its model.

In these cases, you are going to have to find ways to give the user clues about how something works. With graphical interfaces, a common way to solve this problem is with *metaphors*. But not all metaphors are created equal, and it's important to understand *why* metaphors work so you know if you've got a good one.

The most famous metaphor is the "desktop metaphor" used in Windows and the Macintosh (see Figure 4-1). The computer screen behaves something like a real world desk. You have these little folders with little files in them, which you can drag around into trash cans, and cute little pictures of real world objects like printers. To the extent that this metaphor works, it's because the little pictures of folders actually remind people of folders, which makes them realize that they can put documents into them.

FIGURE 4-1

The classic desktop metaphor

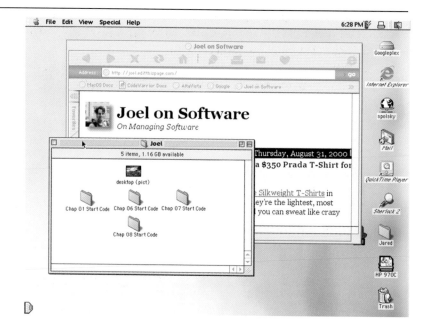

Take a look at Figure 4-2, a screenshot from Kai's Photo Soap. Can you guess how to zoom in?

FIGURE 4-2

Can you guess how to zoom in with Kai's Photo Soap?

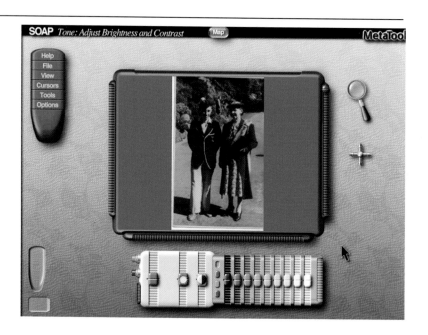

It's not very hard. The magnifying glass is a real world metaphor. People know what magnifying glasses do. And there's no fear that the zoom operation is actually changing the size of the underlying image, since that's not what magnifying glasses do.

A metaphor, even an imperfect one, works a lot better than none at all. Can you figure out how to zoom in with Microsoft Word, as shown in Figure 4-3?

FIGURE 4-3

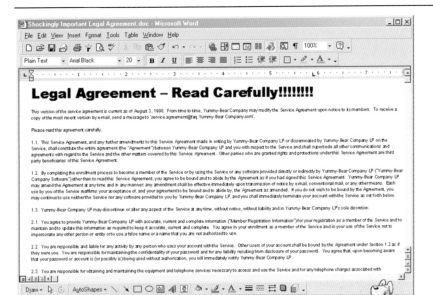

OK, now how do you zoom in with Microsoft Word?

Word has two tiny magnifying glasses in their interface. One of them is on the `Print Preview` button, which actually zooms *out*, and the other is on the `Document Map` button, whatever that is. The actual way to change the zoom level here is with the dropdown box that is currently showing "100%." There's no attempt at a metaphor, so it's harder for users to guess how to zoom. This is not necessarily a bad thing; zooming is probably not important enough in a word processing application to justify as much screen space as Kai gives it. But it's a safe bet that more Kai users will be able to zoom in than Word users.

Affordances

Well-designed objects make it clear how they work just by looking at them. Some doors have big metal plates at arm-level. The only thing you can do to a metal plate is push it. You can't pull it. You can't rotate it. In the words of usability expert Donald Norman, the plate *affords* pushing. Other doors have big, rounded handles that just make you want to *pull* them. They even imply how they want you to place your hand on the handle. The handle *affords* pulling. It makes you *want* to pull it.

Other objects aren't designed so well and you can't tell what you're supposed to do. The quintessential example is the CD jewel case, which requires you to place your thumbs *just so* and pull in a certain direction. Nothing about the design of the box would indicate how you're supposed to open it. If you don't know the trick, it's very frustrating, because the box just won't open.

The best way to create an affordance is to echo the shape of the human hand in "negative space." Look closely at the (excellent) Kodak DC-290 digital camera, shown in Figures 4-4 and 4-5.

FIGURE 4-4

The Kodak DC290 Digital Camera, front view. Notice the rubber grip at left and the rubber nubbin in the lower right.

On the front, you can see a big rubber grip that looks like your right fingers should fit there. Even smarter, on the back in the lower left corner you can see an indent that looks uncannily like a thumbprint. When you put your left thumb there, your left index finger curls snugly on the front of the camera, between the lens and another rubber nubbin. It provides a kind of comforting feeling you haven't felt since you sucked your thumb (and curled your index finger around your nose).

The Kodak engineers are just trying to persuade you to hold the camera with both hands, in a position that ensures the camera will be more stable and even keeps stray fingers from blocking the lens by mistake. All this rubber is not functional; its sole purpose is to encourage you to hold the camera correctly.

Good computer UI uses affordances, too. About ten years ago, most push buttons went "3D." Using shades of grey, they appear to pop out of the screen. This is not just to look cool: it's important because 3D buttons afford pushing. They look like they stick out and they look like the way to operate them is by clicking on them. Unfortunately, many Web sites these days (unaware of the value of affordances) would rather have buttons that look *cool* rather than buttons which look *pushable*; as a result, you sometimes have to hunt around to figure out where to click. Look at the very top of the E*TRADE home page shown in Figure 4-6.

FIGURE 4-5

Back view. See the thumbprint in the lower left?

FIGURE 4-6

The E*TRADE home page. Which parts of the black banner are clickable?

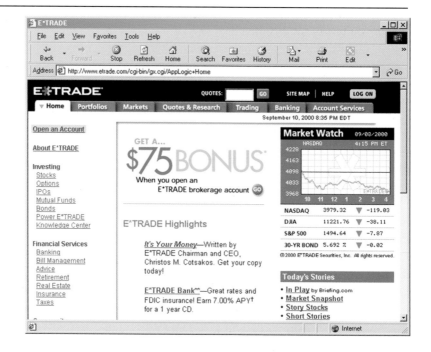

On the black banner at the top, The GO and LOG ON buttons pop out and *look* like you can click on them. The SITE MAP and HELP buttons don't look so clickable; in fact, they look exactly like the QUOTES label, which *isn't* clickable.

About four years ago, many windows started sprouting three little ridges that look like a grip on the lower right corner (see Figure 4-7).

FIGURE 4-7

The grip in the lower right corner affords dragging.

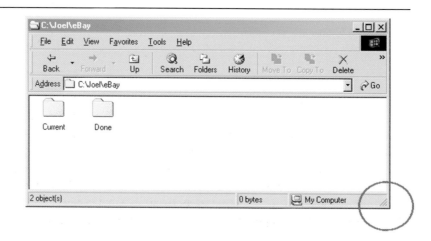

It looks like the kind of thing somebody would put on a slide switch to increase the friction. It *affords* dragging. It just *begs* to be dragged to stretch the window.

Tabbed Dialogs

A problem that seems to vex programmers (especially the ones who neglected to buy this book and read Chapter 3) is dialog boxes with just too many settings to fit on the screen. The only way to deal with this is to create a dialog that changes dynamically. For example, look closely at the Preferences dialog from Netscape Navigator shown in Figure 4-8.

FIGURE 4-8

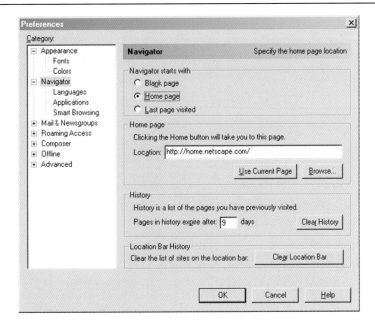

Netscape's way of dealing with too many options.

Now, you and I are elite programming hackers with a lot of experience with these kinds of dialogs. So when we look at Figure 4-8, we immediately understand that choosing one of the categories from the left hand part of the screen is going to magically change which options are available on the right hand part of the screen.

For some reason, this type of indirection was incredibly logical to the programmers who designed it, but many users didn't understand it. The problem? Well, most people are not elite programming hackers.

Most people would never *guess* that choosing something from the list on the left is supposed to change the contents of the dialog on the right: there's no visual reason to think that. In fact, what most people think is that the list on the left is nothing more than another setting, and they are afraid to touch it because it seems like a pretty scary setting that they don't understand.

When you do usability tests with dialogs like that, and you ask people to change one of the settings not actually shown on the main page (in this case, "Navigator"), you'll find that a remarkable number of people just can't figure out how to do it. When Microsoft did a usability test with a similar dialog from an old version of Microsoft Word, only 30% of the users succeeded at the task. A full 70% simply gave up without accomplishing the task they were given.

So, the Microsoft Word team switched to the famous *tabbed dialogs* like the one shown in Figure 4-9.

FIGURE   4-9

Internet Explorer uses tabs.

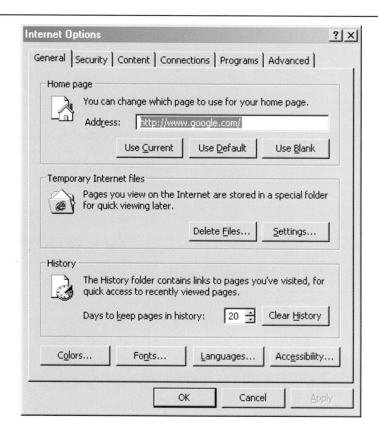

When they tried the tabbed dialogs in the usability lab, usability shot up from 30% to 100%. Let me tell you from experience that there are just not a whole lot of things that you can do that will improve your usability from 30% all the way to *100%*.

Tabbed dialogs are a great affordance. It's really *obvious* from Figure 4-9 that you have six tabs; it's really *obvious* which tab you're on, and it's really *obvious* how to switch to a different tab. Given the remarkable success of this metaphor and the fact that the code for tabbed dialogs is built into modern operating systems and available practically for free, it's a wonder you still see applications that don't take advantage of them. These applications suffer from actual, measurable, real world usability problems because they refuse to get with the program.

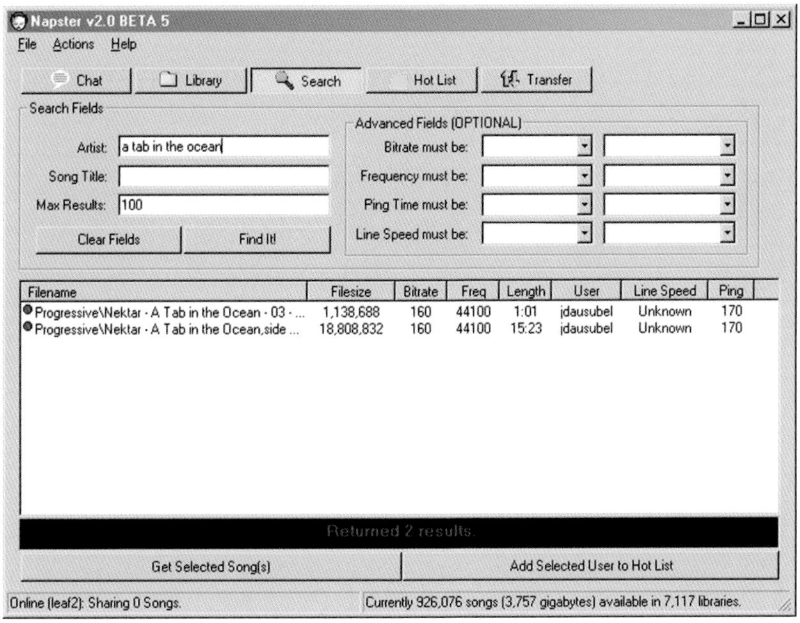

FIGURE 4-10

The Napster 2.0 user interface has five separate screens (Chat, Library, Search, Hot List, and Transfer), and you use the buttons at the top to switch among them. This is an obvious candidate for tabs. Here's the weird thing: the Napster code is actually using the Windows tabbed dialog control, but for some reason, it's running in a funny mode that displays as buttons rather than tabs. So Shawn Fanning, the Napster programmer, could have literally flipped one bit to get a more usable interface.

5

Broken Metaphors

Remember the briefcase from Windows 95? (See Figure 5-1.) That cute little icon that occupied a square inch or so on everybody's desktop for a few years until Microsoft realized that nobody wanted one?

Nobody wanted one because it was a *broken metaphor.* It was supposed to be a "briefcase" where you put files to take home. But when you took the files home, you still had to put them on a floppy disk. So, do you put them in the briefcase or on a floppy disk? I'm not sure. I never could get it to work.

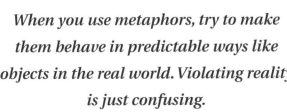

A metaphor badly chosen is worse than no metaphor at all. Unfortunately, desktop user interface designers feel that they're breaking some kind of law if they don't use metaphors, so they would rather pick a wrong metaphor than go without.

When you use metaphors, try to make them behave in predictable ways like objects in the real world. Violating reality is just confusing.

What's the purpose of a metaphor in the first place? To *teach users* what the program model is so that the program model and the user model come into agreement. If you use the wrong metaphor, you are actually teaching the user the *wrong thing* about how the program works, so you're creating more trouble than you're solving. There's some historical evidence that the Windows 95 briefcase metaphor just didn't work: later versions of Windows have tried to compensate for the bad metaphor by forcing you to read a screen full of instructions whenever you drag files into that dang doohickey.

Guess what? Nobody reads instructions. My new Cuisinart food processor must have three hundred stickers on it that say "Do Not Even Think of Operating This Device without Reading the Instructions, and That Means You!" Which, we know as anthropologists, actually means that *millions* of people use Cuisinarts without reading the instructions. I'll go into that more soon. For now, I'd like to talk about *broken metaphors* like the briefcase and what a doggone nuisance they can be.

Obeying Physics

In Chapter 4, I talked about how nifty tabbed dialogs are. Microsoft Excel uses tabs to store multiple sheets in a workbook as shown in Figure 5-2.

FIGURE 5-2

Microsoft Excel uses tabs to show multiple pages.

	A	B	C
	Date	Description	Amount
2	January 4, 1998	Van by the river	$ 303.32
3	February 7, 1998	Cheesy-poofs	$ 933.30
4	March 13, 1998	Pringles	$ 133.25
5	April 16, 1998	Cheesy-poofs	$ 821.13
6	May 20, 1998	Cheesy-poofs	$ 529.58
7	June 23, 1998	Cheesy-poofs	$ 258.88
8	July 27, 1998	Cheesy-poofs	$664.03
9	August 30, 1998	Cheesy-poofs	$ 668.06
10	October 3, 1998	Cheesy-poofs	$ 276.96
11	November 6, 1998	Cheesy-poofs	$ 211.54
12	December 10, 1998	Cheesy-poofs	$760.80
13	January 13, 1999	Cheesy-poofs	$ 46.81
14	February 16, 1999	Pringles	$ 962.60
15	March 22, 1999	Funyuns	$940.62
16	April 25, 1999	Delaware Certificate of Bankrupcy	$ 86.35

Book1

Income \ **Expenses** / Change in Couch

Tabs are kind of small, so people don't necessarily notice them there, but everyone knows how they are expected to work and nobody has trouble using them. For example, in Figure 5-2 it's obvious that the "Income" sheet doesn't live in its own file. It's also obvious that there is no sheet called "Wombats." And it's obvious that the way to see the "Income" sheet is to click on the tab that says "Income." Am I boring you with obvious facts? The great thing about metaphors is that they allow you to "borrow" a part of the user's mental model of the nature of physical objects in the real world.

When you're using metaphors, it's very helpful if the computer program obeys the physical laws of the real world object. Many broken metaphors are the result of a failure to adhere to the "laws of nature," that is, the laws of the real world object that they are emulating.

Consider the ruler in Microsoft Word for Windows—specifically, the three small doohickeys on the left side which control the left indent, the hanging indent, and the first line indent, as circled in Figure 5-3.

FIGURE 5-3

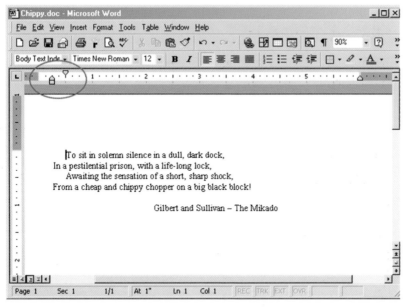

Microsoft Word for Windows has three small, adjustable doohickeys that can be dragged to adjust the paragraph indenting.

People find these a bit hard to use. Here's why: if you drag the top doohickey, which represents the first line indent (as shown in Figure 5-4), only the top doohickey moves. That's what you would expect. But if you drag the bottom doohickey, representing the overall indent, all three doohickeys move, as shown in Figure 5-5. It's not just an inconsistency— it's a violation of the laws of nature! In nature, things are either connected or they're not. If I move my fork, I don't expect the knife and spoon to move, too!

FIGURE 5-4

Dragging the top doohickey moves it. So far so good.

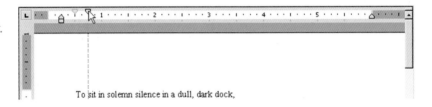

FIGURE 5-5

Dragging the bottom doohickey moves all three, thus violating a "law of nature."

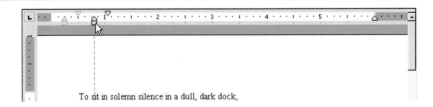

Multiple Rows of Tabs

When I first posted Chapter 4 on the Web, many readers emailed me to say that tabbed dialogs are all well and fine, but they're terrible as soon as you have more than one row of tabs. Indeed, they're right. The biggest problem has to do with the way multiple rows of tabs always seem to violate physics: when you click on a tab from another row, the tabs all shuffle around like restless schoolchildren on Class Photo Day, as shown in Figures 5-6a and 5-6b.

FIGURE 5-6

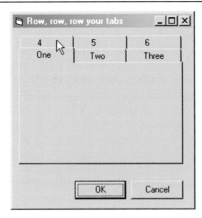 

(a) Click on a tab from the back row…

(b)…and the tabs move around, in a confusing way

This violation of realism is distressing enough that the designers of Microsoft's Visual C++ IDE went to a great deal of trouble to implement scrolling tabs. These have tiny arrows to control which tabs are visible and a neat "torn tab" effect so you notice that there are tabs missing to the right (see Figure 5-7).

FIGURE 5-7

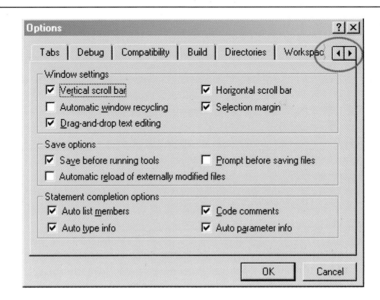

Another way to deal with too many tabs

The real solution to this problem, I think, is to figure out why you have so many options and eliminate a whole bunch, as discussed in Chapter 3. Nobody likes a dialog with a couple dozen tabs, all with cryptic monikers full of complicated options. But if you simply *must* have multiple rows of tabs, at the very least, try not to make them violate physics. With today's faster processors and graphics cards, it's easy to create a simple animation effect so that the front batch of tabs *slides down* when you click on the back row. For an illustration of this, see Figures 5-8a through 5-8d.

FIGURE 5-8

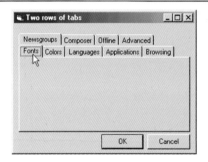

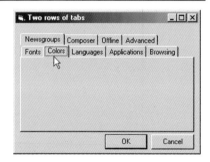

(a) Two rows of tabs.

(b) When you click on a tab from the front row, it behaves as expected

Those Pesky Navigation Tabs

Tabs seem to be pretty popular on Web pages, too. Look at Figure 5-9, the *Urbanfetch* Web site. It's pretty obvious from the appearance of the page that the tabs represent different sections of the Web site.

There are two problems. The first is the slow speed of the Web. I know, it's pretty whiny to complain about the slow speed of the Web. After all, the Web allows you to look at detailed Lego catalogs and find that perfect, tangerine-colored, sloped Lego brick in *seconds*, then have it delivered to your home in twenty-four hours or less—something which used to take several months of research and a painful weeklong excursion in a covered wagon to the nearest big city. But I've gotten spoiled, and for me, the inevitable three-second delay when you click on a page is starting to get pretty annoying. There's an unwritten children's bedtime story in all of this: *The Princess and the High Latency Internet Connection.* In this story, Prince Webby and his mother, the Mouse Queen, convince themselves that the poor child who knocked on their door in a rainstorm is a real princess, because she's used to a personal T-1 line in the castle, and when she's forced to use a 28.8 modem, she *complains* and *complains*…

Anyway. What was I talking about? Oh, yeah. Tabs on a Web page. When you actually click on a tab in a computer program, the screen responds *immediately*, obeying the laws of the real world. But when you click on a tab on a Web page, even a fast Web page, you wait at least three seconds until a *new* page slowly comes up showing you something that is as likely as not to be completely different. When you click on the tab on the *Urbanfetch* Web site in Figure 5-9, five things happen that violate physics:

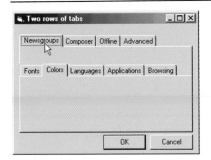 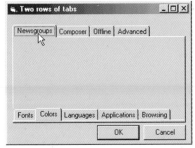

(c) When you click on a tab from the back row, the front row starts to drop down.

(d) After a half-second animation, the front row, still in front, is now at the bottom *of the dialog and the back row is fully revealed.*

1. Nothing happens for a few seconds while the new page is fetched.

2. Then the whole page goes white for a while.

3. Then, finally, a new page appears.

4. But now all the tabs are in a different place (the row of tabs shifts upward due to a lack of attention to detail on the part of the site designers).

5. The whole color scheme has changed now, including the color of the *Urbanfetch* logo, which is not supposed to be a part of the tab area anyway.

Some of these quirks are intrinsic to all Web sites; there's nothing that can be done about latency or the way pages refresh (short of using JavaScript and Dynamic HTML, which isn't quite standard enough yet). And some of these quirks are specific to *Urbanfetch*'s site.

The joke here is that all of these problems with tabs are not really usability problems, despite the fact that some well-known Web usability gurus have complained a lot about them. The site is perfectly usable. Why? Go back to our rule from Chapter 4. The point of a metaphor is to *show the user* the program model. On a Web page, tabs show the user how the site is organized into sections. Once the user clicks, it almost doesn't matter what happens—you've accomplished your goal. (A much worse problem with the site in Figure 5-10 is the various links *below* the row of tabs, which don't look like links and don't look pushable. You would be forgiven if you thought that they were merely advertising slogans and failed to push them.)

FIGURE 5-9

Click on the Electronics tab, wait five seconds...

FIGURE 5-10

...and watch the whole screen shift around and change color. These minor violations of physics do not actually detract from the usability of the site.

Case Study

Microsoft Outlook introduced a new UI concept they called the "Outlook Bar." Located on the left side of the window, it is probably the most confusing part of a rather confusing interface.

Look at Figure 5-11. Yeah, I know, you're dying to see what's in my Inbox, but ignore that for a moment and focus on the left edge of the screen where it says Outlook Shortcuts. Just by looking at it, can you figure out how to use it? What happens if you click on the button that says Outlook Shortcuts? Or the button that says My Shortcuts? Are you supposed to click on them or drag them? Nothing about the visual appearance gives you any clues about how the thing works.

FIGURE 5-11

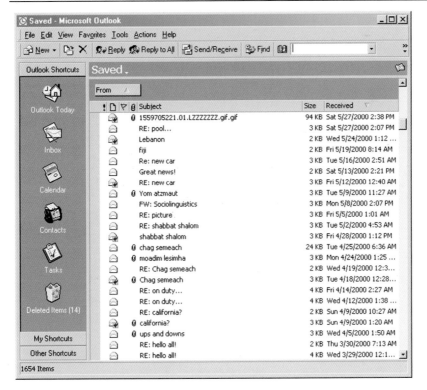

The Outlook Bar. Can you figure out how it works just by looking at it?

Now look at my redesigned version in Figure 5-12. It operates exactly the same way, but it uses a metaphor that provides some subtle visual cues to show how it's supposed to work. `Outlook Shortcuts` looks like a physical card with some icons on it. And it's very clear that `My Shortcuts` and `Other Shortcuts` are additional cards with icons on them, tucked out of the way so that you can see `Outlook Shortcuts`. When you click on one of these additional cards, it slides up to show you its contents.

FIGURE 5-12

My redesigned version of the Outlook Bar uses a real live metaphor to convey to the user how it's supposed to work.

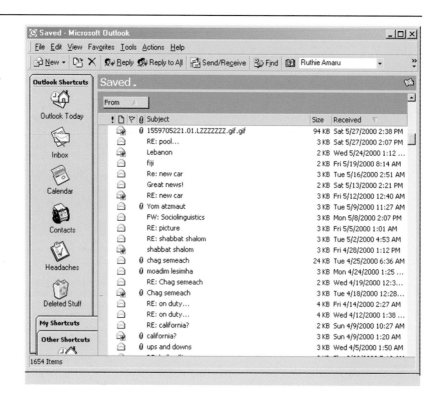

CHAPTER

6

Consistency and Other Hobgoblins

The main programs in the Microsoft Office suite, Word and Excel, were developed from scratch at Microsoft. Others were bought from outside companies, notably FrontPage (bought from Vermeer) and Visio, bought from Visio. You know what FrontPage and Visio have in common? They were originally designed to look and feel just like Microsoft Office applications.

The decision to emulate the Office UI wasn't merely to suck up to Microsoft or to position the companies for acquisition. Indeed, Charles Ferguson, who developed FrontPage, does not hesitate to admit his antipathy for Microsoft; he repeatedly *begged* the Justice Department to *do something* about the Redmond Beasties (until he sold his company to them, after which his position became a lot more complicated). In fact, Vermeer and Visio seem to have copied the Office UI mainly because it was expedient: it was easier and quicker than reinventing the wheel.

When Mike Mathieu, a group program manager at Microsoft, downloaded FrontPage from Vermeer's Web site and tried it out, it worked a whole lot like Word. Since it worked so much like he *expected* a program to work, it was easier to use. The program model matched the user model. When he tried to do things, they *worked*. And this ease of use made him happy and gave him a favorable impression of the program right off the bat.

Now, when Microsoft gets a favorable impression of a program right off the bat, they shell out $150 million or so. Your goal is probably more modest; you want your customers to get a favorable impression and shell out maybe $39. But it's the same idea: consistency *causes* ease of use, which, in turn, *causes* good feelings and results in more money for you.

It's hard to underestimate just how much consistency helps people to learn and use a wide variety of programs. Before GUIs, every program reinvented the very fundamentals of the user interface. Even a simple operation like "exit," which every program had to have, was completely inconsistent. In those days, people made a point of memorizing, at the very least, the exit command of common programs so they could exit and run a program they understood. Emacs fanatics memorized :q! (and nothing else) in case they ever found themselves stuck in vi by mistake, while vi users memorized C-x C-c (Emacs even has its own way to represent control characters). Over in DOS land, you couldn't even use WordPerfect unless you had one of those dorky plastic keyboard templates that reminded you what Alt+Ctrl+F3 did. I just memorized F7, which got me the heck outta there so I could run something intelligent like edlin.

Even tiny inconsistencies in things like the default typing behavior (overwrite or insert) can drive you *crazy*. I've gotten so used to Ctrl+Z meaning "undo" in Windows applications that when I use Emacs I am constantly minimizing the window (Ctrl+Z) by mistake. (The joke of it is, the very reason Emacs interprets Ctrl+Z as *minimize* is for "consistency" with that terrific user interface, csh, the C shell from UNIX.) This is one of those minor frustrations that add up to a general feeling of unhappiness.

To take an even smaller example, Pico and Emacs both use Ctrl+K to delete lines, but with a *slightly* different behavior that usually mauls my document whenever I find myself in Pico. I'm sure you have a dozen examples of your own.

In the early days of Macintosh, before Microsoft Windows, Apple's evangelists told everyone that the average Mac user used more programs to get their work done than the average DOS user. I don't remember the exact numbers, but I believe it was something like one or two programs for the average DOS user versus twelve programs for a Mac user. Because all Mac programs worked the same way, it was easy to learn a new one, so Mac users learned and used a larger number of programs.

Consistency is a fundamental principle of good UI design, but it's really just a corollary of the axiom "make the program model match the user model," because the user model is likely to reflect the way that users see *other* programs behaving. If the user has learned that double-clicking text means *select word*, you can show them a program they've never seen before and they will guess that the way to select a word is to double-click it. And now that program had *better* select words when they double-click (as opposed to, say, looking the word up in the dictionary), or else you'll have a usability problem.

If consistency is so obviously beneficial, why am I wasting your time and mine evangelizing it? Unhappily, there is a dark force out there that fights consistency. That force is the natural tendency of designers and programmers to be creative.

I hate to be the one to tell you "don't be creative," but unfortunately, to make a user interface easy to use, you are going to have to channel your creativity into some other area. In most UI decisions, before you design anything from scratch, you absolutely must look at what other popular programs are doing and emulate that as closely as possible. If you're creating a document-editing program of some sort, it better look an awful lot like Microsoft Word, right down to the accelerators on the common menu items. Some of your users will be used to Ctrl+S for save; some of them will be used to Alt+F,S for save, and still others will be used to Alt,F,S (releasing the Alt key). Another group will look for the floppy disk icon in the top left area of the window and click it. All four had better work or your users are going to get something they don't want. If you think that running the spell-checker should be Ctrl+S, you're going to annoy an awful lot of people who are just trying to save their work.

I've seen companies where management prides themselves on doing things *deliberately* different from Microsoft. "Just because Microsoft does it, doesn't mean it's right," they brag, and then proceed to create a gratuitously different user interface from the one that people are used to. Before you start chanting the mantra "just because Microsoft does it, doesn't mean it's right," please consider two things.

One, even if it's not right, if Microsoft is doing it in a popular program like Word, Excel, Windows, or Internet Explorer, millions of people are going to *think* that it's right, or at least fairly standard. They are going to assume that your program works the same way. Even if you think that Alt+Left is not a good shortcut key for "Back," there are literally millions of people out there who will try to use Alt+Left to go back, and if you refuse to do it on some general religious principle that Bill Gates is the evil Smurf arch-nemesis Gargamel, then you are just gratuitously ruining your program so that you can feel smug and self-satisfied, and your users will *not* thank you for it.

Two, don't be so sure it's not right. Microsoft spends more money on usability testing than you do; they keep detailed statistics based on millions of tech support phone calls; and there's a darn good chance that they did it that way because more people can figure out how to use it that way.

To create a good program with a usable interface you're going to have to leave your religion at the door, thank you. Microsoft may not be the only company to copy: if you're making an online bookstore, you should probably make sure that your Web site is at least semantically the same as Amazon.com. Amazon.com keeps your shopping cart around for ninety days. You might think that you are extra smart and design your program to empty the cart after two hours. If you do this, there will be ex–Amazon.com customers who put stuff in your shopping cart and come back two weeks later expecting it to still be there. When it's gone, you've lost a customer.

If you're making a high-end photo editor for graphics professionals, I assure you that 90% of your users are going to know Adobe Photoshop, so you better behave a heck of a lot like Photoshop in the areas where your program overlaps. If you don't, people are going to say that your program is hard to use even if *you* think it's easier to use than Photoshop, because it's not behaving the way *they* expect it to.

There is another popular tendency to reinvent the common controls that come with Windows. (Don't even get me started about Netscape 6.) There was a time when you could tell which programs were compiled with Borland's C++ compiler because they used big fat OK buttons with giant green checkboxes. This wasn't nearly as bad as Kai's Photo Soap.

Look at Figure 6-1. Fine, so it's stunningly beautiful, but look closely at the exit dialog. To me, the O with a line through it (which actually means "no") reminds me of "OK." The standard on Windows is to have OK on the left, so I wind up hitting the wrong button a lot. The only benefit to having funny symbols instead of "OK" and "Cancel" like everyone else is that you get to show off how *creative* you are. If people make mistakes because of Kai's creativity, well, that's just the price they have to pay for being in the presence of an *artist*. (Another problem with this "dialog" is that it doesn't have a standard title bar to move the dialog around onscreen. If the dialog gets in the way of something you want to see in order to answer the question in the dialog, you are out of luck.)

Now, there's a lot to be gained by having a slick, cool-looking user interface. Good graphic design like Kai is pleasing and will attract people to your program. The trick is to do it *without* breaking the rules. You can change the visual look of dialogs a bit, but don't break the functionality.

When the first version of Juno was written, it had the standard log-on dialog that prompted you for a user name and a password. After you entered the user name, you were supposed to press Tab to go to the password field and type in a password.

FIGURE 6-1

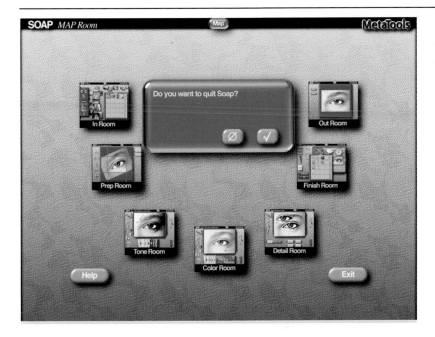

Kai's Photo Soap does everything *differently.*

Now, this distressed one of the managers at Juno who had a lot more experience with UNIX than with Windows. He was used to typing the user name, then pressing Enter to jump to the password field (instead of Tab). When you're writing a program targeted at nonexpert Windows users, a UNIX programmer is probably *not* the ideal example of a typical user. But this manager was very insistent that the Enter key should move to the next field instead of doing the Windows-standard "OK" thing. "Just because Microsoft does it, doesn't mean it's right," he chirped.

So, the programmers spent a remarkable amount of time writing some amazingly complicated dialog-box handling-code to work around the default behavior of Windows. (Being inconsistent is almost always *more* work than simply acting like your platform expects you to act). This code was a maintenance nightmare; it didn't port so well when we moved from 16-bit to 32-bit Windows. It didn't do what people expected. And as new programmers joined the team, they didn't understand why there was this strange subclass for dialogs.

Over the years, an awful lot of programmers have tried to reimplement various common Windows controls, from buttons to scrollbars, toolbars, and menu bars (the Microsoft Office team's favorite thing to reimplement). Netscape 6 goes so far as to reimplement every single common Windows control. This usually has some unforeseen bad effects. The best example is with the edit box. If you reimplement the edit box, there are a lot of utilities that you've never even *heard* of (like Chinese language editing add-ins, and bidirectional versions of Windows that support right-to-left text) that are going to stop working because they don't recognize your nonstandard edit box. Some reviewers of the Netscape 6 preview releases complained that the URL box, using a nonstandard Netscape edit control, does not support common edit control features like right-clicking to get a context menu.

When you find yourself arguing with an anti-Microsoft fundamentalist or a creative graphic designer about consistency, they're apt to quote Ralph Waldo Emerson incorrectly: "Consistency is the hobgoblin of little minds..." Emerson's real quote is "A *foolish* consistency is the hobgoblin of little minds."

Good UI designers use consistency intelligently, and though it may not show off their creativity as well, in the long run it makes users happier.

7

Putting the User in Charge

The history of user interfaces—from the early 1970s when interactive systems first appeared, to today's most modern GUI interfaces—has followed a pendulum. Each generation of user interface designers collectively changes its mind about whether users need to be guided through a program or whether they should be left alone to control the program as they see fit. Following trends in user control is a bit like following the hemlines at the Milan fashion shows. *Plus ça change, plus c'est la même chose.* Here's a bird's-eye view of what happened.

The first computer systems weren't very interactive at all. You created a program by punching holes on eighty-column cards using a giant hole-punching machine that looked like something from the ship in *Lost in Space* and made an incredibly satisfying clacking sound. Of course, there was no way to fill in a hole you made by mistake— so if you made even *one mistake* you had to repunch the whole card. Then you carefully took your deck of cards over to a large machine called a *hopper* and piled the cards in. (It was called a hopper because it would hop all over the floor doing a happy overstuffed-washing-machine dance unless you bolted it down.)

The hopper ate most of your cards, choking on a few, but eventually, begrudgingly, it accepted your program. On a good day, it wouldn't even chew up any of your cards, forcing you to painstakingly repunch them.

Once the hopper successfully choked down your card deck, you walked across campus to the student union and got some lunch. If you lingered a bit in the comic book store after lunch, by the time you got back to the Computer Center your program would have worked its way halfway up the queue. Every ten minutes or so, the computer operator printed out the status of the queue and pinned it up to the bulletin board near the Card Mangler. Eventually your program would run and a printout would appear in your cubbyhole telling you that there was a syntax error on line 32, that it took four seconds of CPU time to run, and that you now had fourteen seconds of CPU time left out of your monthly budget.

Interactive Computing

All of this changed dramatically when the first interactive computer systems started showing up. They introduced the famous *command-line interface* (CLI). You literally sat down, typed a one-line request to the computer, and when you hit the enter key, you *got your response* right then and there. No more time for lunch. No comic books. It was a sad day. When you sat down with a command-line interface, you stared at a prompt. "READY," said some of the systems, "C:\>," said others (that's a picture of an ice-cream cone that fell over). In a fit of stinginess, some systems managed to squeeze their prompt down to one character. "$," said the UNIX shell. Presumably, UNIX programmers had to pay for their computer time *by the letter*.

Now what do you do? Well, that's entirely up to you. You can ask for a listing of files; you can look at the contents of a file; you can run a program to calculate your biorhythms; whatever you want. The method by which you completed tasks as disparate as sending an email or deleting a file was exactly the same: you typed in a previously-memorized command.

The CLI was the ultimate example of an interface where the designer gets out of the way and lets the user do *whatever* they want. CLIs can be easy to use, but they're not very learnable. You basically need to memorize all the frequently used commands, or you need to constantly consult a reference manual to get your work done. Everybody's first reaction to being sat down in front of a CLI is, "OK, *now* what do I do?" A typical computer session from 1974 is shown in Figure 7-1.

Soon another style of interface developed: more of a *question and answer* model. When you sat down to a program, it asked you questions. You never had to remember a thing. See Figure 7-2 for an excellent piece from this period.

FIGURE 7-1

```
$ bio 8/19/1942
bio: not found
$ /usr/local/games/bio
bio: not enough arguments
$ man bio
man: no entry for bio in the manual.
$ /usr/local/games/bio 8/19/1942
bio: not enough arguments
$ /usr/local/games/bio 8 19 1942
bio: there are only 12 months in a year!!!
$ /usr/local/games/bio 1942 8 19
bio: please enter a year between 1900 and 1979
$ /usr/local/games/bio 42 8 19
x
 x
   x
     x
^C
$
```

If you didn't have the manual, you had to guess or ask a guru.

FIGURE 7-2

```
READY
bio

WHAT YEAR WERE YOU BORN?
1942

WHAT MONTH WERE YOU BORN?
AUGUST

WHAT??
AUG

WHAT??
8

WHAT DAY WERE YOU BORN?
 19

WHAT??
19

YOU WERE BORN ON AUGUST 19ST, 191942.

YOU'RE BIORYTHIM IS:

x
 x
  x
  x
   x
^C
STOP.
INTERRUPTED.

1.03 SECONDS CPU TIME USED
READY
```

An excellent example of one of the great, lost interactive computer programs of the early 1970s, reconstructed here from memory. Notice that the program helpfully asks you questions, so you never need to remember a command.

Interface designers of the Middle Command Line Era eventually realized that people didn't want to sit with a manual in their lap to get things done. They created question-and-answer programs, which basically combined the manual with the program itself by showing you what to do as you went along.

Soon, programs starting sprouting more and more features. The silly biorhythm programs sprouted features to tell you what day of the week you were born on. The more serious Star Trek games (where you chased a little Klingon ship around a 10×10 grid) gave you choices: you could fire photon torpedoes *or* move your ship. Pretty soon, the newest innovation was having a menu-driven program. This was thought to be the height of UI coolness. Computer software advertisements bragged about menu-driven interfaces (see Figure 7-3).

FIGURE 7-3

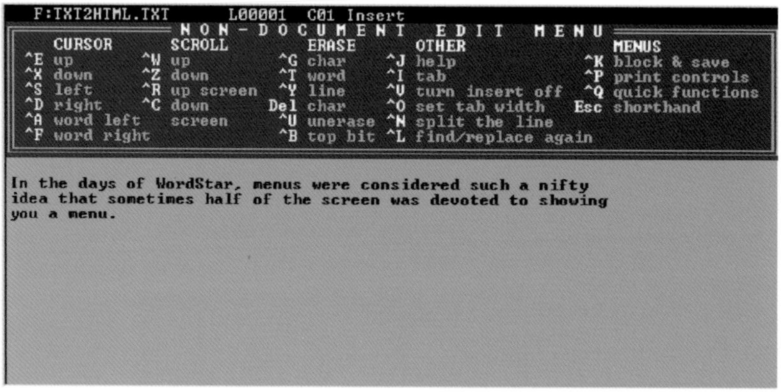

A screenshot from WordStar, a best-seller in 1984.

```
F:TXT2HTML.TXT        L00001   C01  Insert
==================== N O N - D O C U M E N T   E D I T   M E N U ====================
   CURSOR          SCROLL           ERASE           OTHER                MENUS
^E up         ^W up          ^G char      ^J help             ^K block & save
^X down       ^Z down        ^T word      ^I tab              ^P print controls
^S left       ^R up screen   ^Y line      ^U turn insert off  ^Q quick functions
^D right      ^C down        Del char     ^O set tab width    Esc shorthand
^A word left     screen      ^U unerase  ^N split the line
^F word right                ^B top bit  ^L find/replace again

In the days of WordStar, menus were considered such a nifty
idea that sometimes half of the screen was devoted to showing
you a menu.
```

Around the peak of menu-mania, with office workers everywhere trapped in a twisty maze of complicated menus, all alike, an old philosophy swung back into fashion: suddenly, it once again became popular to let the user be in control. This philosophy was sharply expounded by the designers of the original Apple Macintosh who repeated again and again, let the *user* decide what to do next. They were frustrated by the DOS programs of the day, which would get into nasty modes where they *insisted*, no, *demanded* that the user tell them *right now* what file name they want for their new file, even if the user couldn't care less at that moment and really, *really* just wanted to type in that stupid toll-free phone number they saw on TV to order a combination vegetable shredder–clam steamer before they forgot it. In the eyes of the Macintosh designers, menu-based programs were like visiting Pirates of the Caribbean at Disneyland: you had to go through the ride in the exact order that it was designed; you didn't have much of a choice about what to do next; it always took exactly four minutes; and if you wanted to spend a bit *more* time looking at the cool pirates' village, well, you couldn't. Whereas the sleek *new* Macintosh interface was like visiting the Mall of America. Everything was laid out for you, easily accessible, and brightly lit, but you got to make your *own* choices about where to go next. A Macintosh program dumped you in front of a virtually blank white screen where the first thing you did was start poking around in the menus to see what fun commands were available for you. Look! *Fonts*!

This is still how many Windows and Macintosh programs work. But around 1990, a new trend arose: usability testing. All the large software companies built usability labs where they brought in innocent "users," sat them down in front of the software to be tested, and gave them some tasks to do.

Alas, usability testing does not usually test how *usable* a program is. It really tests how *learnable* a program is. As a result, when you plunk a wide-eyed innocent down in front of a typical program they've never seen before, a certain percentage of them will stare at the screen googly-eyed and never even *guess* what it is they are supposed to do. Not all of them. Teenagers will poke around at random. More experienced computer users will immediately start scanning the menus and generally *gefingerpoken und mittengrabben* around the interface and they'll soon figure it out. But some percentage of people will just sit there and fail to accomplish the task.

This distresses the user interface designers, who don't like to hear that 30% of the "users" failed to complete the task. Now, it probably shouldn't. In the real world, those "users" either (a) wouldn't have to use the program in the first place because they are baristas at coffee shops and never use computers; or (b) wouldn't have to use the program in the first place because they aren't project managers and they don't *use* project management software; or (c) would get somebody to teach them how to use the program, or would read a manual or take a class. In any case, the large number of people that fail usability tests because they don't know where to start tends to scare the heck out of the UI designers.

So what do these UI designers do? They pop up a dialog box like the one in Figure 7-4.

FIGURE 7-4

The first screen you see when you run Microsoft Power-Point. Almost anyone could figure out how to open and create files using the menu commands; this dialog really only helps absolute beginners.

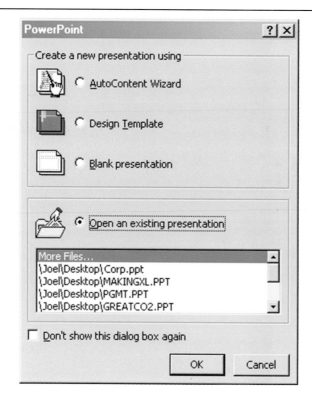

As it turns out, the problems people were having in usability tests motivated Karen Fries and Barry Saxifrage, talented UI designers at Microsoft, to invent the concept of *wizards*, which first appeared in Microsoft Publisher 1.0 in 1991. A wizard is a multipage dialog that asks you a bunch of questions in an interview format and then does some large, complicated operation based on your answers. Originally, Fries conceived of the wizard as a *teacher* that merely taught you how use the traditional menu-and-dialog interface. You told it what you wanted to do and the wizard actually demonstrated how to do it using the menus. In the original design, there was even a speed control to adjust how fast the wizard manipulated the menus: at its highest speed, it basically just did the work for you without showing you how to do it.

The wizard idea caught on like wildfire, but not the way Fries envisioned it. The teaching functionality rapidly went out the door.

More and more designers started using wizards simply to work around real and perceived usability problems in their interface. Some wizards were just out of control. Intuit's wizard for creating a new company with their *QuickBooks* accounting package seems to go on for *hundreds* of screens and asks you questions (like your employee's social security numbers) that you aren't likely to know the answers to right now but would be happy to input later. The Windows team

FIGURE 7-5

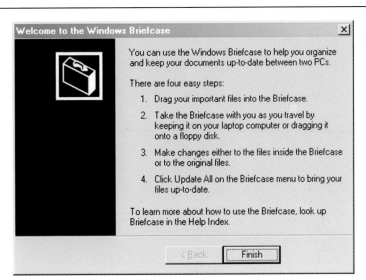

The Windows team liked wizards so much that they went a bit overboard making some degenerate, one-screen wizards with a vestigial Back button that is perpetually greyed out.

decided that wizards were so cool that they created wizards for *everything*, even some silly one-screen-long wizards (see Figure 7-5).

The thing about wizards is that they're not *really* a new invention, they're just a fashionable swing back to guiding people through things step-by-step. The good thing about taking people by the hand like this is that when you usability test it, it works. The bad thing about taking people by the hand is that if they have unusual needs or if they want to do things in a different order than you conceived, they get frustrated by the maze you make them walk through.

I think it's time to find a happy middle. As humane designers, we need to remember to let users be in charge of their environment; control makes people happy. A modern word processor is perfectly happy to let you type all your text without any formatting, then go back and reformat it. Some people like to work this way. Other people like to have every word appear on screen in its final, formatted form. They can do this, too.

CHAPTER

8

Design for Extremes

Consider if you will a simple key.

Nothing fancy, just your ordinary house key.

Is a key easy to use? It might seem so. On a sunny day, when a sixteen-year-old lad with sharp eyes comes home from soccer practice, puts his key in the lock and turns it, it sure *seems* usable enough.

But later that day, Dad comes home carrying two big bags of groceries in his arms. He has to fumble a bit before the key goes into the lock, and eventually he drops the left bag and oranges go rolling all over the front porch, to the delight of the neighbor's dog, who starts barking and yipping and running around and generally being a nuisance.

Then, when Grandpa comes to visit, his hands shake a little and it takes him almost a minute to get the key into the lock. By the time Mom gets home, it's dark and nobody turned on the damn *porch light* so it's very hard to see where the slot is.

Good usability doesn't just mean "usability under the best of circumstances." It means usability under as many adverse circumstances as possible. This is a principle called *design for extremes*. Don't design something that can only be read in daylight: design it to be read in dim light, too. Don't design something that can only be handled by a strong, seventeen-year-old athlete; design something that an arthritic person can use as well. Design things that work outdoors, in the rain, when you're not looking, when you didn't read the manual, when you're distracted by bombs falling around you, or volcanic ash, or when you've got both arms in a cast and can't quite turn your head.

One day a man named Sam Farber was watching his wife peel apples for a tart. She had mild arthritis, so the process was slightly painful. Sam called his friend Davin Stowell who had started a design firm in New York City called Smart Design and together they came up with the idea for a line of kitchen products that would be more comfortable for people who suffered from arthritis. They made hundreds of models of handles using wood and Styrofoam. They tried them on all kinds of people. Eventually they honed in on the design that was comfortable for almost everybody.

Arthritis is a joint inflammation that can cause swelling and pain. Sam's products have big handles that are easier to grip than the usual pencil-thin variety. They are ergonomically designed to fit into human hands comfortably. The handles are made of a soft, black rubber

FIGURE 8-1

A cheese slicer and a cheese grater made by OXO International. Originally designed for arthritis sufferers, it seems that everybody likes using OXO Good Grips tools.

called Santoprene, which means you don't have to squeeze tightly to keep them from slipping; even a weak grasp is enough. The handles have a soft, bristly rubber area near the top where you can grip them comfortably with your thumb and forefinger. This makes the handle even less slippery, especially when it's wet.

One in seven people suffer some form of arthritis—that's almost forty million people in the United States alone. Designing a line of products for just that market niche was likely to succeed. Indeed, Farber's company, OXO International, became a stunning success. But their market is not just people with arthritis: *everybody* likes OXO products. They are simply *more pleasant* to use.

Back to the problem of keys. When you design a key-entry system, you can't just design it for optimal conditions. You have to design it so that it is easy to use when your hands are full, when it's pitch dark, when your hands are shaking, or when the teenager from next door puts superglue in the lock to get back at you for telling his parents about the big party he had while they were in Jamaica.

Having trouble imagining such a system? I think that proximity cards—colloquially known as card keys—come pretty close. If you haven't seen one, it's a small card the size of a credit card but a little bit thicker. When you wave it within about six inches of a scanner mounted next to the door, it releases a mechanical lock, usually magnetic, and you can push the door open. You can keep a card key in your pocket, and when you get near enough to the door—voila, it opens. It works better under extreme conditions (well, maybe not power failures), but, more importantly, *everybody* finds a card key easier to use than a normal key, even under the best of conditions.

1. *Design for extremes so that your product can be used under extreme conditions, and*

2. *Design for extremes so that your product is more comfortable to use under normal conditions.*

Designing with these ideas in mind is called *respecting the user*, which actually means not having much respect for the user. Confused? Let me explain.

What does it mean to make something *easy to use*? One way to measure this is to see what percentage of real world users are able to complete tasks in a given amount of time. For example, suppose the goal of your program is to allow people to convert digital camera photos into a Web photo album. If you sit down a group of average users with your program and ask them all to complete this task, then the more *usable* your program is, the higher the percentage of users who will be able to successfully create a Web photo album.

To be scientific about it, let's get one hundred real world users together in a room. They are not necessarily familiar with computers. They have many diverse talents. Some are world famous ballerinas. Others can herd cats. Some are nuclear engineers, others are world-class morons.

Many of these people emphatically do *not* have talents in the computer area. Others might be good at computers, but they are distracted when they try to use your program. The phone is ringing. WHAT? The baby is crying. WHAT?! The cat keeps jumping on the desk and batting around the mouse. The computer mouse, I mean. I CAN'T HEAR YOU!

Now, even without going through with this experiment, I can state with some confidence that some of the users will simply fail to complete the task or will take an extraordinary amount of time doing it. I don't mean to say that these users are *stupid*. Quite the contrary, they are probably highly intelligent. Or maybe they are accomplished cello players, or whatever, but as far as *you're* concerned, they are just not applying all of their motor skills and brain cells to your program. You're only getting about 30% of their attention, so you must make do with a user who, from inside the computer, does not appear to be playing with a full deck.

I haven't talked about software for a while. When you're designing for extremes with software, the three most important "extremes" to remember are:

1. Design for people who can't read.

2. Design for people who can't use a mouse.

3. Design for people who have such bad memories they would forget their own *name* if it weren't embossed on their American Express.

These are important enough that they each merit a chapter.

9

People Can't Read

When you design user interfaces, it's a good idea to keep two principles in mind:

1. Users don't have the manual, and if they did, they wouldn't read it.

2. In fact, users can't read anything, and if they could, they wouldn't want to.

These are not, strictly speaking, *facts*, but you should act as if they are facts, for it will make your program easier and friendlier.

Users don't read the manual.

First of all, they may not actually *have* the manual. There may not *be* a manual. If there is one, the user might not have it for all kinds of logical reasons: they're on a plane; they're using a downloaded demo version from your Web site; they're at the beach and the manual is at work; their IS department never *gave* them the manual. Even if they have the manual, frankly, they are not going to read it unless they absolutely have no other choice (and maybe not even then). With *very* few exceptions, users will not cuddle up with your manual and read it through before they begin to use your software. In general, your users are trying to get something *done*, and they see reading the manual as a waste of time, or at the very least, a distraction that keeps them from getting their task done.

The very fact that you're reading this book puts you in an elite group of highly literate people. Yes, I know, people who use computers are by and large able to read, but I guarantee you that a good percentage of them will find reading a chore. The language in which the manual is written may not be their first language, and they may not be totally fluent. They may be kids! They can decipher the manual if they really *must*, but they sure ain't gonna read it if they don't have to. Users do just-in-time reading on a strictly need-to-know basis.

The upshot of all this is that you probably have no choice but to design your software so it doesn't need a manual in the first place. The only exception I can think of is if your users do not have any *domain knowledge*—they don't really understand what the program is intended to do, but they know that they better learn. A great example of this is Intuit's immensely popular small-business accounting program, QuickBooks. Many people who use this program are small-business owners who simply have no idea what's involved in accounting. The manual for QuickBooks assumes this and assumes that it will have to teach people basic accounting principles. There's no other way to do it. If a small business owner wants to learn accounting, they actually might just curl up with the QuickBooks manual in a comfortable chair and read it cover to cover. Still, for people who do understand accounting, QuickBooks is reasonably easy to use without the manual.

In fact, users don't read anything.

This may sound a little harsh, but you'll see when you do usability tests that there are quite a few users who simply do not read words that you put on the screen. If you pop up an error box of any sort, they simply will not read it. This may be disconcerting to you as a programmer because you imagine yourself conducting a *dialog* with the user. "Hey, user!" you say. "You can't open that file, we don't support that file format!" Still, experience shows that the more words you put on a dialog box, the fewer people will actually read it.

The fact that users do not read the manual leads many software designers to assume that they are going to have to educate users by verbosely describing things as they go along. You see this all over the place in programs. In principle it's OK, but in reality, people's aversion to reading means that this will almost always get you in trouble. Experienced UI designers literally try to *minimize* the number of words in dialogs to increase the chances that they will get read. When I worked on Juno, the UI people understood this principle and tried to write short, clear, simple text. Sadly, the CEO had been an English major at an Ivy League college; he had no training in UI design or software engineering, but he sure *thought* he was a good editor of prose. So, he vetoed the wording done by the professional UI designers and added a lot of his own verbiage. A typical dialog in Juno looks like the one shown in Figure 9-1. Compare that to the equivalent dialog in Microsoft Windows shown in Figure 9-2.

Intuitively, you might guess that the Juno version, with eighty words of instructions, would be "superior" (in other words, easier to use) than the Windows version with its five words of instructions. In reality, when you run a usability test on this kind of thing, you'll find that:

1. Advanced users skip over the instructions. They assume they know how to use things and don't have time to read complicated instructions.

2. Most novice users skip over the instructions. They don't like reading too much and hope that the defaults will be OK.

3. The few novice users who do earnestly try to read the instructions (some of whom are only reading them because it's a usability test and they feel obliged) are often confused by the sheer number of words and concepts. So, even if they were pretty confident that they would be able to use the dialog when it first came up, the instructions actually *confused them even more.*

Lesson number one is that if you're an English major from a fancy university, then you are in a whole different *league* of literacy than the average Joe and you should be very careful about wording dialogs that seem like they might be helpful to *you.* Shorten it, dumb it down, simplify, get rid of the complicated clauses in parentheses, and do usability tests. But do *not* write things that look like Ivy League faculty memos. Even adding the word "please" to a dialog, which may seem helpful and polite, will slow people down: the increased bulk of the wording is going to reduce, by some measurable percentage, the number of people who try read the text.

FIGURE 9-1

The modem dialog from Juno 4.0. Nobody reads these things.

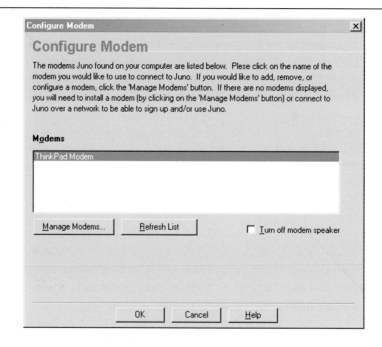

FIGURE 9-2

The equivalent dialog from Microsoft Windows. Although it contains far fewer words, it's much more usable.

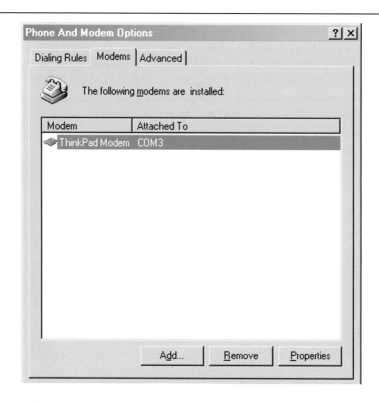

Another important point is that *many people are intimidated by computers.* You probably know this, right? But you may not realize the implications of this. I was watching a friend try to exit Juno. For some reason, she was having quite a bit of trouble. I noticed that when you try to exit Juno, a dialog pops up, as shown in Figure 9-3, saying "Thanks for using Juno. Are you sure you want to exit?"

FIGURE 9-3

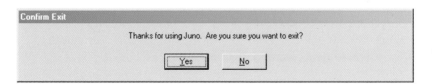

The Juno exit confirmation dialog doesn't get read, either.

She was hitting No, and then she was kind of surprised that Juno hadn't exited. The very fact that Juno was questioning her choice made her immediately assume that she was doing something wrong. Usually, when programs ask you to confirm a command, it's because you're about to do something that you might regret. She had assumed that if *the computer* was questioning her judgment, then *the computer* must have been right, because, after all, computers are *computers,* whereas she was merely a *human,* so she hit No.

Is it too much to ask people to read eleven lousy words? Well, apparently. First of all, since exiting Juno has no deleterious effects, Juno should have just exited without prompting for confirmation, like every other GUI program on the planet. But even if you are *convinced* that it is *crucial* that people confirm before exiting, you could do it in two words instead of eleven, as shown in Figure 9-4. Without the completely unnecessary "Thank you" and the remorse-inspiring "Are you *sure?*" this dialog is a lot less likely to cause problems. Users will certainly read the two words, say "um, duh?" to the program and pound the Yes key.

FIGURE 9-4

Two words are much more likely to be read than eleven.

Sure, you say, the Juno Exit Confirmation dialog trips up a *few* people, but is it *that* big a deal? Everyone will *eventually* manage to get out of the program. But herein lies the difference between a program that is *possible* to use versus a program that is *easy* to use. Even smart, experienced, advanced users will appreciate things that you do to make it easy for the distracted, inexperienced, beginner users. Hotel bathtubs have big grab bars. They're just there to help disabled people, but everybody uses them anyway to get out of the tub. They make life easier, even for the physically fit.

In the next chapter, I'll talk a bit about the mouse. Just as users can't or won't read, users are not very good at using the mouse either, so, you have to accommodate them.

10

People Can't Control the Mouse

When the Macintosh was young, Bruce "Tog" Tognazzini wrote a regular column in Apple's developer magazine on UI design. In his column, people wrote in with lots of interesting UI design problems, which he discussed. These columns continue to this day on his Web site (http://www.asktog.com). They've also been collected and embellished in a couple of great books like *Tog on Software Design* (Addison-Wesley, 1995), which is a lot of fun and a great introduction to UI design, and *Tog on Interface* (Addison-Wesley, 1992).

Tog invented the concept of the *mile-high menu bar* to explain why the menu bar on the Macintosh, which is always glued to the top of the physical screen, is so much easier to use than menu bars on Windows, which appear *inside* each application window. When you want to point to the File menu on Windows, you have a *target* about half an inch wide and a quarter of an inch high to acquire. (The term "acquiring a target" comes from gunnery.) You must move and position the mouse rather precisely in both the vertical and the horizontal dimensions. See Figure 10-1. (While I was preparing this screen shot, Rocky, the Office Assistant, was trying to bust loose. Please don't let that distract you. He has been apprehended and returned to his rightful place scratching himself in the corner of the screen.)

FIGURE 10-1

On Windows computers, each window has its own menu bar. To acquire the "File" menu, for example, you have a target that is about 30 × 15 pixels in size.

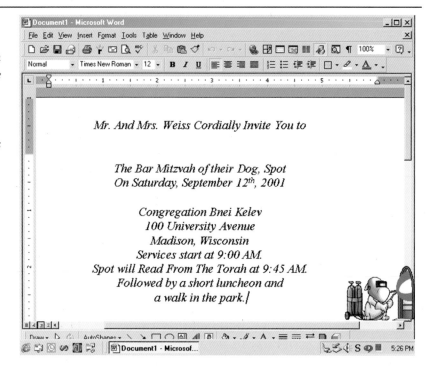

FIGURE 10-2

On the Macintosh, the menu bar is snug at the top of the screen, so the target is 30 × infinity pixels in size.

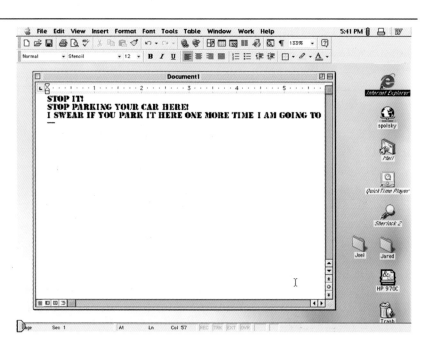

But on a Macintosh, you can slam the mouse up to the top of the screen without regard to how high you slam it, and it will stop at the physical edge of the screen—the correct vertical position for using the menu. Effectively, you have a target that is still half an inch wide, but a mile high. Now you only need to worry about positioning the cursor horizontally, not vertically, so the task of clicking on a menu item is that much easier.

Based on this principle, Tog has a pop quiz: what are the five spots on the screen that are easiest to acquire (point to) with the mouse? The answer: all four corners of the screen (where you can literally slam the mouse in one fell swoop without any pointing at all), plus the current position of the mouse, because it's already there.

The principle of the mile-high menu bar is fairly well known. However, it must not be entirely obvious because the Windows 95 team missed the point *completely* with the Start push-button, which sits *almost* (but not *exactly*) in the bottom left corner of the screen. In fact, it's about two pixels away from the bottom and two pixels from the left of the screen. So, for the sake of a couple of pixels, Tog writes, Microsoft literally "snatches defeat from the jaws of victory" and makes it that much harder to acquire the Start button. It could have been a mile square, absolutely *trivial* to hit with the mouse. For some reason, I don't know why, it's not. Even five years later, after many major releases of Windows, nobody has bothered to fix the Start button to make it easier to hit.

In the previous chapter, we talked about how users hate reading and will avoid it unless they absolutely cannot accomplish their task. Similarly:

Users can't control the mouse very well.

I don't mean this literally. What I mean is, you should design your program so that it does not require a tremendous amount of mouse-agility to use correctly. The top six reasons for this are:

1. Some people use suboptimal pointing devices, such as track-balls, touchpads, and the little red thingy on a ThinkPad, all of which are harder to control than standard mice.

2. Sometimes people use mice under bad conditions: on a crowded desk; with a dirty trackball that makes the mouse skip; or with a mouse that is just a five-dollar clone and doesn't track properly.

3. Some people are new to computers and have not yet developed the motor skills to use mice accurately.

4. Some people will literally never have the motor skills to use mice precisely. They may be very young or very old; they may have arthritis, tremors, carpal tunnel syndrome; or they may suffer from any number of disabilities.

5. Many people find that it is extremely difficult to double-click without moving the mouse slightly. As a result, they often drag things around on their screen when they mean to launch applications. You can often spot these people by their messy desktops because half the time they try to launch something, they wind up moving it instead.

6. Even in the best of situations, using the mouse a lot *feels slow* to people. If you force people to perform a multistep operation using the mouse, they may feel like they are being stalled, which in turn makes the UI feel unresponsive. This, as you should know by know, makes people unhappy.

In ye olden days, when I worked on Excel, laptops didn't come with pointing devices built in, so Microsoft made a clip-on trackball that clipped to the side of the keyboard. A normal mouse is controlled with the wrist and most of the fingers. This is much like writing, and you probably developed very accurate motor skills for writing in elementary school. But a trackball is controlled entirely with the thumb. As a result, it's much harder to control a trackball to the same degree of accuracy as a mouse. Most people find that they can control a mouse to within one or two pixels but can only control a trackball to within three or four pixels. On the Excel design team, I always urged people to try out their new UIs with the trackball instead of only with a mouse, to see how it would feel to people who are not able to move the mouse exactly where they want it.

One of the great UI crimes against humanity is the dropdown list-box, shown closed and then open in Figure 10-3.

Think about how many detailed mouse clicks it will take to choose, say, Wingdings. First, you must click on the down arrow to make the list appear. Then, using the scroll bar, you must carefully scroll until Wingdings appears in view. Many of these dropdowns are carelessly designed to show only two or three items at a time, so this scrolling is none too easy, especially if you have a lot of fonts. It involves either carefully dragging the position indicator (with such a small range of

FIGURE 10-3

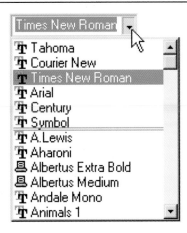

The dropdown list-box in its normal state and expanded.

movement, it's probably unlikely that this will work); or clicking repeatedly on the second down arrow; or trying to click in the area between the thumb and the down arrow—which will eventually stop working when the thumb gets low enough, annoying you even further. Finally, if you do manage to get Wingdings into view, you have to click on it. If you miss, you get to start all over again. Now multiply this process by ten if, say, you want to use a fancy font for the first letter in each of your chapters. Then you're *really* unhappy.

The poxy dropdown listbox is even more annoying because there's such an easy solution: just make the dropdown part high enough to show all of the options at once. Ninety percent of the combo boxes out there don't even use all the available space to drop down, which is a *sin*. If there is not enough room between the main edit box and the bottom of the screen, the dropdown should grow *up* until it fits all the items, even if it has to go all the way from the top of the physical screen to the bottom. And then, if there are still more items than there's room for, it should scroll automatically as the mouse approaches the edge rather than requiring the poor user to mess with a teensy weensy scrollbar.

Furthermore, don't make me click on the little tiny arrow to the right of the edit box before you pop up the dropdown—let me click *anywhere* on the edit box! This expands the click target about tenfold and makes it that much easier to acquire the target with the mouse pointer.

Let's look at another problem with mousing: edit boxes. You may have noticed that almost every edit box on the Macintosh uses a **really fat, bold font** called Chicago, which looks kind of ugly and distresses graphic designers to no end. Graphic designers (unlike UI designers) have been taught that thin, variable spaced fonts are more gracious, look better, and are easier to read. All this is true. But graphic designers learned their skills on *paper*, not on the screen. When you need to *edit* text, monospaced text (that is, text in which every letter is the same width) has a major advantage over variable spaced fonts: it's easier to see and select narrow letters like 'l' and 'i'. I learned this lesson after watching a sixty-year-old man in a usability test painfully trying to edit the name of his street, which was something like Fillmore Street. We were using 8-point Arial font, so the edit box looked like Figure 10-4.

FIGURE 10-4

When you use a font like 8-point Arial or the Windows default MS Sans Serif, lowercase 'L's are only one pixel wide.

Notice that the 'I' and the 'L's are literally *one pixel wide*. The difference between a lowercase 'l' and a lowercase 'I' is literally *one pixel*. (Similarly, it is almost impossible to see the difference between 'RN' and 'M' in lowercase, so this edit box might actually say Fillrnore.)

There are very few people who would notice if they mistyped Flilmore or Fiilmore or Fillrnore, and even if they did, they would have a *heck* of a time trying to use the mouse to select the offending letter and correct it. In fact, they would even have a hard time using the blinking cursor, which is two pixels wide, to select a single letter. Look at Figure 10-5 to see how much easier it would have been if we had used a fat font (shown here as Courier Bold).

OK, so it takes up more space and doesn't look as cool to your graphic designers. Deal with it! It's much easier to use. It even *feels* better, because as the user types, they get sharp, clear text. And it's so much easier to edit when you have a typo.

FIGURE 10-5

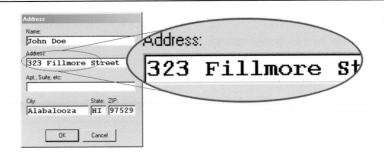

A larger, mono-spaced, bold font like Courier is a lot easier to edit.

Snap to Border

Here's a common programmer thought pattern: there are only three numbers: 0, 1, and *n*. If *n* is allowed, all *n*'s are equally likely. This thought pattern comes from the old coding convention (probably smart) that you shouldn't have any numeric constants in your code except for 0 and 1. (Constants other than 0 and 1 are referred to as "magic numbers." I don't even want to get into the psychology of *that*.)

For example, programmers tend to think that if your program allows you to open multiple documents, it must allow you to open *infinite* documents (as memory allows), or at least 2^{32}, the only magic number programmers concede. A programmer would tend to look with disdain on a program that limited you to twenty open documents. "*Twenty?!* Why twenty? It's not even a power of two!"

Another implication of *all n's are equally likely* is that programmers tend to think that if users are allowed to resize and move windows, they should have *complete* flexibility over where these windows go, right down to the last pixel. After all, positioning a window two pixels from the top of the screen is "equally likely" as positioning a window *exactly* at the top of the screen.

But it's not true. As it turns out, it's *not* equally likely. There are many good reasons why you might want a window exactly at the top of the screen (it maximizes screen real estate), but there really aren't any reasons to leave two pixels between the top of the screen and the top of the window. So, in reality, 0 is much more likely than 2.

The programmers over at Nullsoft, creators of WinAmp, managed to somehow avoid the programmer-think that has imprisoned the rest of us for a decade. WinAmp has a great feature. When you start to drag the window *near* the edge of the screen (coming within a few pixels), it automatically *snaps* to the edge of the screen perfectly, which is probably exactly what you wanted since 0 is so much more likely than 2.

The Juno main window has a similar feature: it's the only application I've ever seen that is "locked in a box" on the screen and cannot be dragged beyond the edge. This is a great idea. What are the chances that you really wanted your application to be hanging halfway off the screen? You lose a little bit of flexibility, but in exchange, you get a user interface that recognizes that precisely controlling the mouse is hard, so why should you have to? This innovation (which every program could use) eases the burden of window management in an intelligent way.

Look closely at your program's user interface and give us all a break. Pretend that we are gorillas or maybe smart orangutans and that we have trouble with the mouse. Then, design your interface so that it's good enough to *gesture* with the mouse instead of controlling it precisely like a surgeon's scalpel, and we'll be much more productive.

CHAPTER

11

People Can't Remember

One of the early principles of GUI interfaces was that you shouldn't ask people to remember things that the computer could remember. In the really, really old days of command-line interfaces, if you wanted to open a file, you had to type its name (see Figure 11-1).

The classic example of not relying on people's memory is the Open File dialog box, which shows people a list of files rather than

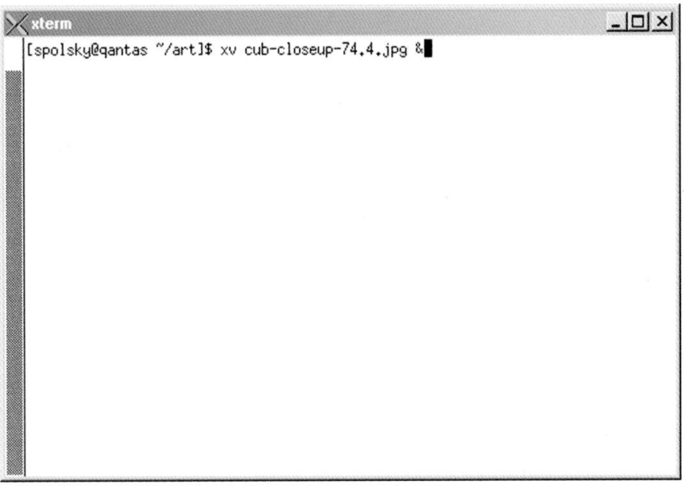

FIGURE 11-1

Opening a file the command-line way. You have to remember that "xv" is the command that displays a picture, and you have to remember the file name.

The figure shows an xterm window with:
```
[spolsky@qantas ~/art]$ xv cub-closeup-74.4.jpg &
```

asking them to recall and type the exact file name. People remember things a lot better when they are given some clues, and they'd always rather choose something from a list than recall it from memory. See Figure 11-2.

FIGURE 11-2

Opening a file the Windows way. You can choose the picture from a list of files.

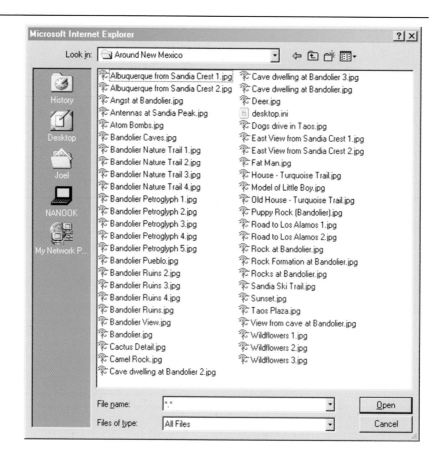

Things got even better when Windows 98 introduced thumbnails. Now you can see small versions of your pictures, which make it even easier to find the one you want, as shown in Figure 11-3.

Another example is the menus themselves. Historically, providing a complete menu of available commands replaced the old command-line interfaces where you had to memorize the commands you wanted to use. This is, fundamentally, the reason why command-line interfaces are simply *not* better than GUI interfaces, no matter what your UNIX friends tell you. Using a command-line interface is like having to learn the complete Korean language just to order food in the Seoul branch of McDonalds. Using a menu-based interface is like being able to

FIGURE 11-3

*Opening a file with
thumbnails. This is
a lot easier than
remembering the
names you gave to
all of your files.*

point to the food you want and grunt and nod your head: it conveys the same information with no learning curve.

You can also see the minimum-memory principle at work in features like autocompletion. When you need to type something, some programs make educated guesses about what you're about to type, as shown in Figure 11-4. In this example, as soon as you type M, Excel guesses that you are likely to be typing Male, because you've typed Male before in this column and proposes that word as the auto-completion. But the ale is *preselected* so that if you didn't *mean* to type Male, you can continue typing (perhaps ystery) and overwrite Excel's guess with no lost effort.

FIGURE 11-4

Autocompletion

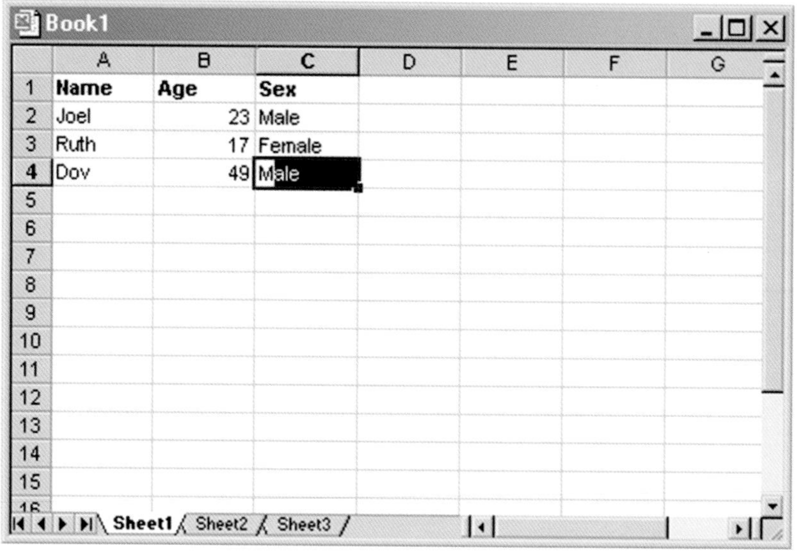

Microsoft Word gets a bit carried away in guessing what you are about to type, as anybody that has ever used this product during the merry month of May has discovered (see Figure 11-5).

Designing for People Who Have Better Things to Do with Their Lives, Redux

One good way to test the usability of a program or dialog you've never seen before is to act a little stupid. Don't read the words on the dialog. Make random assumptions about what things do without verifying. Try to use the mouse with just one finger. (No, not *that* finger). Make lots of mistakes and generally thrash around. See if the program does what you want, or at least, gently guides you instead of blowing up. Be impatient. If you can't do what you want right away, give up. If the UI can't withstand your acting immature and stupid, it could use some work.

In the preceding chapters, I've brought up three principles:

1. Users don't read stuff (Chapter 9).

2. Users can't use the mouse (Chapter 10).

3. Users can't remember anything (this chapter).

FIGURE 11-5

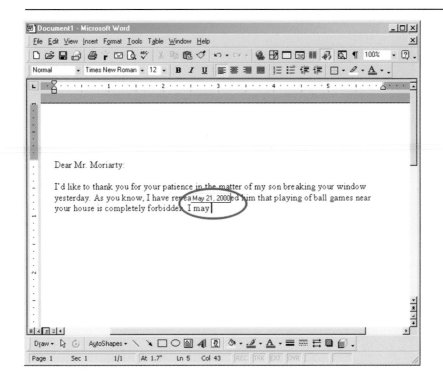

Autocompletion taken too far

"Joel," you say, "admit it. You just think that users are dolts. Why don't you just tell us to design programs for dolts and get on with our lives?"

But it's not true! Disrespecting users is how arrogant software like Microsoft Bob gets created (and dumped in the trash bin), and nobody is very happy.

Still, there is a much worse kind of arrogance in software design: the assumption that "my software is so damn cool, people are just going to have to warp their brains around it." This kind of *chutzpah* is pretty common in the free software world. Hey, Linux is free! If you're not smart enough to decipher it, you don't deserve to be using it!

Human aptitude tends towards the bell curve. Maybe 98% of your customers are smart enough to use a television set. About 70% of them can use Windows. 15% can use Linux. 1% can program. But only 0.1% of them can program in a language like C++. And only 0.01% of them can figure out Microsoft ATL programming.

The effect of this sharp drop-off is that whenever you "lower the bar" by even a small amount, making your program, say, 10% easier to use, you *dramatically* increase the number of people who can use it by, say, 50%.

CHAPTER

12

The Process of Designing a Product

We've talked about the principles of good design, but principles only give you a way to evaluate and improve an existing design. So, how do you figure out what the design should be in the first place? Many people write big, functional outlines of all the features they have thought up. Then they design each one and hang it off of a menu item (or Web page). When they're done, the program (or Web site) has all the functionality they wanted, but it doesn't *flow* right. People sit down and don't know what it does, and they don't know how to use it to accomplish what they want.

Microsoft's solution to this is something called Activity-Based Planning. (As far as I can tell, this concept was introduced to Microsoft by Mike Conte on the Excel team who got bored with that and went on to a second career as a race car driver). The key insight is to figure out the *activity* that the user is doing and then make it easy to accomplish that activity. This is best illustrated with an example.

You've decided to make a Web site that lets people create greeting cards. Using a somewhat naïve approach, you might come up with the following list of features:

1.   Add text to card.

2.   Add picture to card.

3.   Get predesigned card from library.

4.   Send card:

    a.   Using email

    b.   By printing it out

For lack of any better way of thinking about the problem, this might lead itself to a typical Macintosh user interface circa-1985: a program that starts out with a blank card and includes menu items for adding text and pictures, for loading cards from a library, and for sending cards. The user is going to have to browse through the menus trying to figure out what commands are available and then figure out how to put these atomic commands together to create a card.

Activity-based planning is different. Activity-based planning says that you need to come up with a list of *activities* that users might do. So, you talk to your potential users and come up with this "Top Three" list:

1.   Birthday Greeting

2.   Party Invitation

3.   Anniversary Greeting

Now, instead of thinking about your program like a programmer (in terms of, *which features do you need to provide in order to make a card*), you're thinking about it like the user, in terms of *what activities the user is doing*, specifically:

1.   Sending a birthday card

2.   Planning a party, and inviting people to it

3.   Sending an anniversary card

Suddenly, all *kinds* of ideas will rush into your head. Instead of starting with a blank card, you might start with a menu like this:

What do you want to do?

☑   Send a birthday card.

❑   Send an anniversary card.

❑   Send a party invitation.

❑   Start with a blank card.

Users will suddenly find it *much* easier to get started with your program without having to browse through the menus since the program will virtually lead them through the steps to complete the activity. (There is a risk that if you don't pick the activities correctly, you will alienate or confuse users who might have been able to use your program to, say, send a Hanukkah card but don't see that as a choice. So be careful in picking activities that blanket the majority of the market you want to target.)

Just looking at our list of three activities suggests some great features that you might want to add. For example, if the user is sending a birthday or anniversary card, they might want to be reminded next year to send a card to the same person...so you might add a checkbox that says "remind me next year." And a party invitation needs a way to RSVP, so you might add a feature that lets them collect RSVPs from people electronically. Both of these feature ideas came from looking at the *activity* that users were performing instead of the *features* in the application.

This example is trivial; for any serious application, the rewards of activity-based planning are even greater. When you're designing a program from scratch, you already have a vision of what activities your users are going to be doing. Figuring out this vision is not hard at all, it takes almost no effort to brainstorm with your colleagues, write down a list of potential activities, and then decide which ones you want to focus on. The simple act of listing these activities on paper will help your overall design enormously.

Activity-based planning is even more important when you are working on version 2 of a product that people are already using. Here, it may be a matter of observing some of your existing customers to see what they are using your program to accomplish.

In the early days of Excel, up to about version 4.0, most people at Microsoft thought that the most common user activity was doing financial "what-if" scenarios, such as changing the inflation rate to see how it affects profitability.

When we were designing Excel 5.0, the first major release to use serious activity-based planning, we only had to watch about five customers using the product before we realized that an enormous number of people just use Excel to keep *lists*. They are not entering any formulas or doing any calculation at all! We hadn't even considered this before. Keeping lists turned out to be far more popular than any other activity with Excel. And this led us to invent a whole *slew* of features that make it easier to keep lists: easier sorting; automatic data entry; the AutoFilter feature, which helps you see a slice of your list; and multi-user features, which let several people work on the same list at the same time while Excel automatically reconciles everything.

While Excel 5.0 was being designed, Lotus had shipped a "new paradigm" spreadsheet called Improv. According to the press releases, Improv was a whole new generation of spreadsheet, which was going to blow away everything that existed before it. For various strange reasons, Improv was first available on the NeXT, which certainly didn't help its sales, but a lot of smart people believed that Improv would be to NeXT as VisiCalc was to the Apple II: it would be the *killer app* that made people go out and buy all new hardware just to run one program.

Of course, Improv is now just a footnote in history. Search for it on the Web and the only links you'll find are from over-organized storeroom managers who have, for some sick reason, made a Web site with an inventory of all the stuff in their closet collecting dust.

Why? Because in Improv, it was almost impossible to just make *lists*. The Improv designers thought that people were using spreadsheets to create complicated multi-dimensional financial models. Turns out, if they had asked people, they would have discovered that making lists was vastly more popular than multi-dimensional financial models. And in Improv, making lists was a downright chore, if not impossible. Oops.

So, activity-based planning is helpful in the initial version of your application where you have to make guesses about what people want to do. But it's even more helpful when you're planning the upgrade because you understand what your customers are doing.

Another example from the Web is the evolution of Deja.com, which started out as a huge, searchable index of Usenet called *DejaNews*. The original interface basically had an edit box that said "search Usenet for *blah*," and that was it. In 1999, a bit of activity-based planning showed that one common user activity was researching a product or service of the "which dishwasher should I buy" nature. *Deja* was completely reorganized and today it is more of a product-opinion research service: the Usenet searching ability is almost completely hidden. This annoyed the small number of users who were using the site to search for whether their Matrox video card worked with Windows 2000, but it delighted the much larger population of users who just wanted to buy the best digital camera.

The other great thing about activity-based planning is that it lets you make a list of what features you *don't* need. When you create *any* kind of software, the reality is that you will come up with three times as many features as you have time to create. And one of the best ways to decide which features get done and which features get left out is to evaluate *which features support the most important user activities.*

When you are struggling to cut features, having a detailed list of activities you want to support is going to make it much easier. And it's a great way to convince crabby old Marge that her beloved lint-removal feature isn't really worth spending time on.

Imaginary Users

The best UI designers in the industry may bicker among themselves, but they all agree on one thing: you have to invent and describe some imaginary users before you can design your UI. You may remember back in Chapter 1 when I introduced an imaginary user named Pete.

Pete is an accountant for a technical publisher who has used Windows for six years at the office and a bit at home. He is fairly competent and technical. He installs his own software; he reads PC Magazine; and he has even programmed some simple Word macros to help the secretaries in his office send invoices. He's getting a cable modem at home. Pete has never used a Macintosh. "They're too expensive," he'll tell you. "You can get a 733 MHz PC with 128 Meg RAM for the price of..." OK, Pete. We get it.

When you read this, you can almost *imagine* a user. I could also have invented quite another type of user:

Patricia is an English professor who has written several well-received books of poetry. She has been using computers for word processing since 1980, although the only two programs she has ever used are Nota Bene (an ancient academic word processor) and Microsoft Word. She doesn't want to spend time learning the theory of how the computer works, and she tends to store all her documents in whatever directory they would go in if you didn't know about directories.

Obviously, designing software for Pete is quite different from designing software for Patricia, who, in turn, is quite different from Mike, a sixteen-year-old who runs Linux at home, talks on IRC for hours, and uses no "Micro$oft" software.

When you invent these users, thinking about whether your design is appropriate becomes much easier. For example, a lot of programmers tend to overestimate the ability of the typical user to figure things out. Whenever I write something about command-line interfaces being hard to use, I get the inevitable email barrage saying that command-line interfaces are ultra-powerful because you can do things like `gunzip foo.tar.gz | tar xvf -`. But as soon as you have to think about getting Patricia to type "`gunzip...`" it becomes obvious that *that* kind of interface just isn't going to serve her needs, ever. Thinking about a "real" person gives you the empathy you need to make a feature that serves that person's need. (Of course, if you're making Linux backup software for advanced system administrators, you need to invent a character like "Frank" who refuses to touch Windows, which he only refers to as an "operating system" while making quotation marks in the air with his fingers; who uses his own personally modified version of `tcsh`; and who runs X11 with four tiled `xterms` all day long. And about 11 `xperfs`.)

Designing good software takes about six steps:

1. Invent some users.

2. Figure out the important activities.

3. Figure out the *user model*—how the user will expect to accomplish those activities.

4. Sketch out the first draft of the design.

5. Iterate over your design again and again, making it easier and easier until it's well within the capabilities of your imaginary users.

6. Watch real humans trying to use your software. Note the areas where people have trouble, which are probably areas where the program model isn't matching the user model.

Watch Out for Unintended Consequences

One of the most famous UI metaphors of all time is the trash can from the Macintosh desktop. The original metaphor was terrific: when you dragged a file to the trash can, it was deleted. And the neat thing was, you could look in the trash can and see all your old deleted files! So if you ever dragged something there by mistake, you could get it back. How do you get a deleted file back? You drag it out of the trash can, of course! An excellent metaphor (see Figure 12-1).

There was one problem. After a few releases, the Mac designers went a little too far and decided that a trash can with something in it should look "stuffed," so when you drag something in there, you get a full trash can instead of an empty trash can. The trouble is that neat freaks were distracted by the full trash can. It looks *messy*. When they wanted to clean up, they would empty the trash. Over time, many people got into the habit of dragging things to the trash can and then mechanically *emptying* the trash so that the trash can wouldn't look messy, thus defeating its original purpose: to provide a way to get things back!

FIGURE   12-1

The Macintosh trashcan, bane of neat freaks everywhere

The moral of this story: spend a few hours quietly watching real users in their real environment; there's a lot you can learn. I'll talk more about this in the next chapter.

13

Those Pesky Usability Tests

Many software companies have usability testing labs. Here's the theory behind a usability lab. (To those of you who have done tests in a usability lab before, I *must* ask that you *please* try to refrain from snickering and outright guffaws until I get to the end of the theory, please. I'll get to the reality soon enough.)

A Story of Silicon Jungle

One fine day, Eeny the Elephant is lumbering through the jungle when he hits upon a great idea. "Everybody tried B2C and *that* didn't work," thinks Eeny. "Then they tried B2B, and all those companies are in the dumpster, too! The answer is obvious: B2A!"

Eeny quickly raises $1.5 million in seed financing from a friendly group of largish birds who promise a mezzanine round of "five at twenty with preferred warrants" and starts his company. After hiring a couple dozen executives with experience at places like failed dehydrated-hamburger chains and mustache-waxing drive-ins, he finally gets around to hiring a Chief Technology Orangutan (CTO), who, at least, is smart enough to realize that "That Really Cool but Top Secret B2A Company" (as it's now known) is going to need some UI designers, software architects, Directors of Technical Research, usability testing engineers, and, "oh, maybe one or two actual programmers? If we have any stock options left, that is."

So, the architects and UI designers get together and design the software. They make nice storyboards, detailed functional and technical specifications, and a schedule with elegant Gantt and PERT charts that fills an entire wall. Several million dollars later, the programmers have actually built the thing, and it looks like it's actually working. It's on time and under budget, too! In theory. But this story *is* the theory, not the reality, remember?

"That Really Cool, etc." (as it's now known) has hired usability engineers who have spent the last six months building a state-of-the-art usability testing lab. The lab has two rooms: one for observers, with a one-way mirror that allows them to spy on the other room where the "participants" sit. (The usability testers have been warned not to call users "users," because users don't like being called users. It makes them feel like drug addicts.) The participants sit down at a computer with several video cameras recording their every move while they attempt to use The Product.

For a few weeks, a steady stream of mysterious visitors representing all walks of life and most of the important phyla come to the "That Really, etc." campus to take part in the usability tests. As the "participants" try out the software, the usability testers take detailed notes on their official-looking clipboards. The test lasts a couple of weeks while the programmers take a well-deserved, all-expenses-paid rest in Bali to "recharge the ol' batteries" and maybe get tans for the first time in their young, dorky lives.

After about three weeks of this, the Chief Tester of Usability (CTU) emerges from the lab. A hush comes over the company cafeteria (free gourmet lunches). All eyes are on the CTU, who announces, "The results of the usability test will be announced next Tuesday." Then she retreats back into her lab. There is an excited hubbub. What will the results be? Eeny can hardly wait to find out.

The next Tuesday, the entire staff of "That, etc." (as it's now known) have gathered in the company cafeteria to hear the all-important usability results. The programmers are back from the beach, freshly scrubbed and sunburned, wearing their cleanest Star Trek-convention T-shirts. Management arrives dressed identically in Gap pleated khakis. The marketing team hasn't been hired yet. (Don't argue with me, it's my story, and in *my* story we don't hire marketing until we have a product).

The tension is palpable. When the CTU comes into the room, the excitement is incredible. After a tense moment fumbling with Power Point and trying to get the LCD projector to work (surprise! it doesn't work the first time), the results of the usability test are finally presented.

"We have discovered," says the CTU, "that 73% of the participants were able to accomplish the main tasks of the product." A cheer goes up. Sounds pretty good! "However, we've discovered that 23.3% of the users had difficulty or were completely unable to check their spelling and make much-needed corrections. The usability team recommends improving the usability of the spell checker." There are a few other problems, too, and the designers and programmers take detailed notes in their identical black notebooks.

The Chief Code Compiling and Programming Officer (C3PO) stands up. "Well, looks like we've got our work cut out for us, boys and girls!" The programming team, looking earnest and serene, files out of the cafeteria to get back to their dual Pentium workstations and *fix those usability problems!*

Well!

A Bitter Descent into Reality

"In theory there is no difference between theory and practice. In practice there is," as Yogi Berra probably didn't say. Unless you've been working at a big software company, you may have never seen an actual usability lab. The reality of usability testing is really quite different from the theory.

You Don't Need to Test with a Lot of Users

In Chemistry Lab back in high school, the more times you repeated your experiment, the more precise the results were. So, your intuition would probably tell you that the more people you bring in for usability tests, the better.

As it turns out, with a usability test, you don't really care about statistics. The purpose of a usability test is simply to find the flaws in your design. Interestingly, in real life, if you have major usability problems, it only takes about five or six people before you find them. Usability testers have long since discovered that the marginal number of usability problems that you find drops off sharply after the sixth tester and is virtually zero by the twelfth user. This is not science here; it's digging for truffles. Take about 3 or 4 pigs out to the forest, let them sniff around and you'll find most of the truffles. Bringing out 1024 pigs is not going to find any more truffles.

You Usually Can't Test the Real Thing

It's a common sport among usability pundits to make fun of software teams that don't leave enough time in the schedule to do usability tests, change things in response, and retest. "Build one to throw away!" say the pundits.

Pundits, however, don't work in the real world. In the real world, software development costs money, and schedules are based on real world problems (like trying to be first to market, or trying to complete a fixed-budget project on time before it becomes a money-losing proposition). *Nobody has time to throw one away, OK?* When the product is done, we have to ship it ASAP. I've never seen a project where it is realistic to do a usability test on the final product and then open up the code again to fix problems.

Given the constraints of reality, it seems like you have three choices:

1. You can test the code long before it's complete. It may crash too often, and it's unlikely to reflect even the current understanding of what the final product is going to look like, so the quality of the usability results may be limited.

2. You can test a prototype. But then you have to build the prototype, which is almost never easier than building the final product. (Sometimes you can build a prototype faster using a rapid development tool like Visual Basic, while your final product is in C++. Let me clue you in—if you can build working prototypes faster than you can build the real code, you're using the wrong tools.)

3. You can test the code when it's done, then ignore the results of the test because you have to rush the code out to market.

None of these approaches is very satisfactory. I think that the best times to do usability tests are as follows:

4. Do hallway usability tests, also known as "fifty-cent usability tests," when you first design a new feature. The basic idea is that you just show a simple drawing or screen shot of your proposed design to a few innocent bystanders (secretaries and accountants in your company make good victims), and ask them how they would use it.

5.   Do full-blown usability tests *after* you ship a version of your product. This will help you find a whole slew of usability problems to fix for the next version.

The Joel Uncertainty Principle

The Joel Uncertainly Principle holds that:

> *You can never accurately measure the*
> *usability of a software product.*

When you drag people into a usability lab to watch their behavior, the *very act of watching their behavior* makes them behave differently. For example, they tend to read instructions much more carefully than they would in real life. And they have performance anxiety. And the computer you're testing them on has a mouse when they're used to a trackball. And they forgot their reading glasses at home. And when you ask them to type in a credit card number, they're reading a fake credit card number off a sheet you gave them, not off a real credit card. And so on and so forth.

Many usability testers have tried to ameliorate this by testing users "in their natural setting," in other words, by following them home with a zoom-lens spy camera and hiding behind a bushy bougainvillea. (Actually, it's more common just to sit behind them at their desk at work and ask them to "go about their usual activities.")

Usability Tests Are Too Rigged

In most usability tests, you prepare a list of instructions for the user. For example, if you were usability testing an Internet access provider, you might have an instruction to "sign up for the service." (I have actually done this very usability test several times in my career.)

So far, so good. The first user comes in, sits down, starts signing up for the service, and gets to the screen asking them how they want to pay. The user looks at you helplessly. "Do I gotta pay for this *myself?*"

"Oh wait," you interrupt. "Here, use this fake credit card number."

The sign-up procedure then asks if they would like to use a regular modem, a cable modem, or a DSL line.

"What do I put here?" asks the user. Possibly because they don't know the answer, but possibly because they know the answer for *their* computer, only they're not *using* their computer, they're using *yours*, which they've never seen before, in a usability lab, where they've never been before. So you have no way of knowing whether your UI is good enough for this question). At Juno, we knew that the dialog in Figure 13-1 was likely to be the source of a lot of confusion. People certainly had a lot of trouble with it in the lab, but we weren't quite sure if that was because they didn't understand the dialog or if they just didn't know how the lab computer was set up. We even tried telling them "pretend you're at home," but that just confused them more.

FIGURE 13-1

The dialog that we couldn't figure out how to usability test.

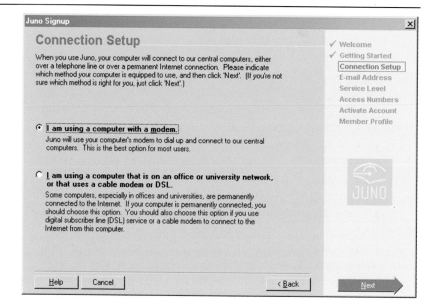

Five minutes later, the program asks for the user's address, and then it crashes when they put in their zip code because of a bug in the early version of the code that you're testing. You tell the next person who comes in, "when it asks for your zip code, don't type anything in."

"OK, sure boss!" But they forget and type the zip code anyway, because they're so used to filling out address forms onscreen from all the crap they've bought on the Web.

The next time you do the usability test, you're determined to prevent these problems. So you give the user a nice, step-by-step, detailed list of instructions, which you have carefully tested so they will work with the latest development build of the software. Aha! Now, suddenly you're *not doing a usability test.* You're doing something else. Charades.

Theatre of the Macabre. I don't know what it is, but it's not a *usability test* because you're just telling people exactly what to do and then watching them do it.

One solution to this problem has been to ask people to bring in their own work to do. With some products (maybe word processors), that's possible, although it's hard to imagine how you could get someone to test your exciting new mailing list feature if they don't need a mailing list. But with many products there are too many reasons why you can't get a realistic usability test going "in the lab."

Usability Tests Are Often Done to Resolve an Argument

More than half of the usability tests I've been involved in over my career have been the result of an argument between two people about the "best" way to do something. Even if the original intent of the usability test was innocent enough, whenever two designers (or a designer and programmer, or a programmer and a pointy-haired manager) get into a fight about whether the OK button should be on the left or the right of the Cancel button, this dispute is inevitably resolved by saying, "we'll usability test it!"

Sometimes this works. Sometimes it doesn't. It's pretty easy to rig a usability test to show the righteousness of one side or the other. When I was working on the Microsoft Excel team, and I needed to convince the Visual Basic team that object-oriented programming was "just as easy" as procedural programming, I basically set up a usability test in which some participants were asked to write cell.move and other participants were asked to write move(cell). Since the audience for the usability test was programmers anyway, the success rates of the non-object-oriented group and the object-oriented group were— surprise, surprise—indistinguishable. It's great what you can prove when you get to write the test yourself.

In any case, even if a usability test resolves a dispute, it doesn't do it in any kind of a statistically valid way. Unless you test thousands of people from all walks of life under all kinds of conditions, something that not even Microsoft can afford to do, you are not actually getting statistically meaningful results. Remember, the real strength of usability tests is in finding truffles—finding the broken bits so you can fix them. Actually looking at the results as if they were statistics is just not justified.

Some Usability Test Results I Might Believe:

- Almost nobody ever tried right-clicking, so virtually nobody found the new spell-checking feature.

- 100% of the users were able to install a printer the new way; only 25% could install the printer the old way.

- There were no problems creating a birthday card.

- Several participants described the animated paper clip as "unhelpful" and "getting in the way."

- Many people seemed to think that you had to press "Enter" at the end of every line.

- Most participants had difficulty entering an IP address into the TCP/IP control panel because the automatic tabbing from field to field was unexpected.

Some Usability Test Results I Would Not Believe:

- When we used brighter colors, 5% more participants were able to complete the tasks. (Statistically insignificant with such a small sample, I'm afraid).

- Most participants said that they liked the program and would use it themselves if they operated their own steel forge. (Everybody says that in a usability test. They're just being nice, and they want to be invited back to your next usability test.)

- Most participants read the instructions carefully and were able to assemble the model airplane from Balsa wood right the first time. (They're only reading the instructions because you told them to.)

- 65% of the people took more than four and a half minutes to complete the task. (Huh? It's those precise numbers again. They make me think that the tester doesn't get the point of usability tests. *Truffles! We're looking for truffles!*)

Usability Tests Create Urban Legends

My last employer's software was a bit unusual for a Windows program. In addition to the usual File ➤ Exit menu item that has been *totally standard* on all GUI programs since about 1984, this program had an Exit menu at the top level menu bar, visible at all times (see Figure 13-2). When you consider that closing windows is probably the *only* thing in Microsoft Windows that nobody has trouble with, I was a bit surprised that this was there. Somehow, every other Windows program *on the planet* manages without a top-level Exit menu.

FIGURE 13-2

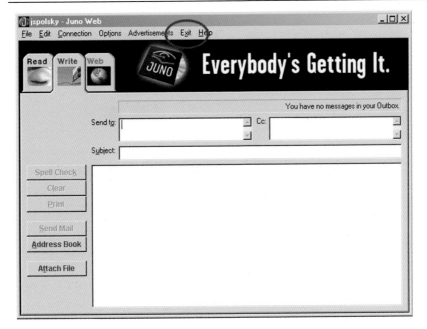

Huh? What's that doing there?

Well, Exit menus don't just *spontaneously* appear. I asked around. It turned out that when the product was first designed, they had actually done some kind of marketing "focus groups" on the product, and for some reason, the *one* thing that everybody remembered from the focus group was that there were people who didn't know how to exit a Windows program. Thus, the famous Exit menu. But the urban legend about this focus group lasted far longer than it should have. For years after that, nobody had the guts to take out the Exit menu.

Most software organizations do usability tests pretty rarely, and—worse—they don't retest the improvements they made in response to the test. One of the risks of this is that some of the problems observed in the test will grow into urban legends repeated through generations of software designers and achieve a stature that is completely disproportional to their importance. If you're a giant corporation with software used by millions of people and you usability test it every few months, you won't have this problem. In fact, if you even bother to *retest* with the changes you made, you won't have this problem (although nobody ever manages to find time to do this before their product has to ship). Microsoft tested so many doggone versions of the Start button in Windows 95 that it's not even funny, and people would *still* come into usability labs not realizing that they were supposed to click on it to start things. Finally, the frustrated designers had to insert a big balloon, which basically said, "Click Me, You Moron!" (see Figure 13-3). The balloon doesn't make Windows any more *usable*, but it does increase the success rate in the usability *test*.

FIGURE 13-3

If you obsess about getting a 100% success rate on your usability test, you can probably force it, but it hardly seems worth the effort. (Somebody who doesn't even know to click the button isn't likely to understand what's going on when they do.)

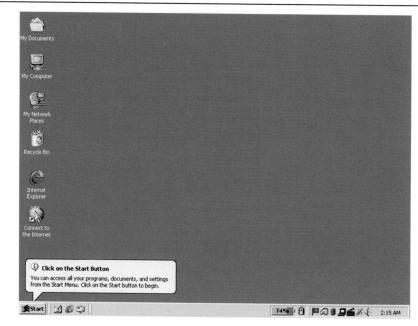

A Usability Test Measures Learnability, Not Usability

It takes several weeks to learn how to drive a car. For the first few hours behind the wheel, the average American teenager will swerve around like crazy. They will pitch, weave, lurch, and sway. If the car has a stick shift, they will stall the engine in the middle of busy inter-sections in a truly *terrifying* fashion.

If you did a usability test of cars, you would be forced to conclude that they are simply unusable.

This is a crucial distinction. When you sit somebody down in a typical usability test, you're really testing how *learnable* your interface is, not how *usable* it is. Learnability is important, but it's not every-thing. Learnable user interfaces may be extremely cumbersome to experienced users. If you make people walk through a fifteen-step wizard to print, people will be pleased the first time, less pleased the second time, and downright ornery by the fifth time they go through your rigmarole.

Sometimes all you *care* about is learnability: for example, if you expect to have only occasional users. An information kiosk at a tourist attraction is a good example; almost everybody who uses your inter-face will use it exactly once, so learnability is much more important than usability. But if you're creating a word processor for professional writers, well, now usability is more important.

And that's why, when you press the brakes on your car, you don't get a little dialog popping up that says, "Stop now? (Yes/No)."

One of the Best Reasons to Have a Usability Test

I'm a programmer. You may think I'm some kind of (sneer) computer book writer or usability "guru," but I'm not. I spend most of my time at work actually writing lines of code. Like most programmers, when I encounter a new program, I'm happy to install it and try it out. I download tons of programs all the time; I try out every menu item and I poke around every nook and cranny, basically playing. If I see a button with a word I don't understand, I punch it. Exploring is how you learn!

A very significant portion of your users are scared of the darn computer. It ate their term paper. It may eat *them* if they press the wrong button. And although I've always known this *intellectually*, I've never really *felt* this fear of the computer.

Until last week. You see, last week I set up the payroll for my new company. I have four people to pay, and the payroll company has set me up with a Web-based interface in which I enter payroll information. This interface has a suctionlike device directly hooked up to vacuum money straight out of my bank account.

Yow.

Now *this* Web site is scary. There are all kinds of weird buttons that say things like "MISC (99) DEDUCTION." The funny thing is, I even *know* what a MISC (99) DEDUCTION is—because I called up to ask them—but I have no idea whether the deduction should be in dollars, hours, negative dollars, or what, and the UI doesn't tell me, and it's not in the help file anywhere. (Well, the help file *does* say "Enter any MISC (99) deductions in the MISC (99) DEDUCTION box," in the grand tradition of help files written by people who don't know any more about the product than what they can figure out by looking at it.)

If this were just a word processor or a bitmap editor, I'd just try it and see what happens. The trouble is, this is a vacuum-cleaner-like device programmed to suck money *directly* out of *my bank account*. And due to the *extreme* incompetence of the engineers who built the site, there is no way to find out what's going on until it's too late: the money has been sucked out of my bank account and direct-deposited into my employees' accounts and I don't even find out what happened until *the next day*. If I type 1000, thinking it means dollars, and it really meant hours, then I'll get $65,000 sucked out of my account instead of $1000.

So, now I know what it feels like to be one of those ordinary mortals who will not do something until they understand it *fully*.

Programmers, on the whole, are born without a lot of sympathy for how much trouble ordinary people have using computers. That's just the way of the world. Programmers can keep nineteen things in their short-term memory at once; normal people can keep about five. Programmers are exceedingly rational and logical, to the point of *exasperation;* normal people are emotional and say things like "my computer hates me." Programmers know how hierarchical file systems work and think they are a neat metaphor; many normal people don't understand how you could have a folder inside a folder. They just don't.

One of the best, if not the *only*, good reason to have a usability test is because it's a great way to educate programmers about the real world. In fact, the more you can get people from your engineering team involved in the usability tests, the better the results. Even if you *throw away* the "formal" results of the test. And that's because one of the greatest benefits of a usability test is to hammer some reality into your engineer's noggins about the real world humans who use their product. If you do usability tests, you should *require* every member of the programming team (including designers and testers) to participate in some way and observe at least some of the participants. Usually this is pretty amusing to watch. The programmers have to sit on their hands behind one-way glass as the user completely fails to figure out the interface they just coded. "Right there, you moron!" the programmer shouts. "The damn CLEAR button, right under your ugly pug nose!" Luckily, the room is soundproof. And the programmer, chastened, has no choice but to come to grips with reality and make the interface *even easier.*

Needless to say, if you outsource your usability test to one of those friendly companies that does all the work for you and returns a nice, glossy report in a three-ring binder, you're wasting your money. It's like hiring someone to go to college for you. If you're thinking of doing this, I suggest that you take the money you would have spent on the usability test and mail it directly to me. I accept Visa, MasterCard, and American Express. For $100,000, I'll even send you a three-ring binder that says, "get rid of the Exit item on the main menu bar."

14

Relativity: Understanding UI Time Warps

When you write software, you have to remember three rules:

1.   Days are seconds.

2.   Months are minutes.

3.   Seconds are hours.

Confused? Don't worry. I'll explain in a minute. But first, a book review.

In 1956, Robert A. Heinlein, the Grand Master of science fiction, wrote a book for boys called *Time for the Stars*. It's been a long time since I read it, but here's what I remember. A fairly mysterious organization called the "Long Range Foundation" is planning an interstellar space trip at a velocity pretty close to the speed of light to search out new planets to colonize. In order to communicate between Earth and the rocket, they can't use radio, of course, because it would be limited to the speed of light, and therefore too slow. So, they decide to use mental telepathy, which, as we all know, is not restricted to the speed of light.

Silly enough? It gets better. The Long Range Foundation carefully selects two twin brothers, Tom and Pat, who have tested very highly on the ESP test. They send one brother away on the spaceship while the other stays home on Earth. And now the ship can communicate with Earth simply by using mental telepathy between the brothers. Great!

Now, here's the educational bit. Since the spaceship is traveling near the speed of light, time *passes slower* on the spaceship. So when Tom (or was it Pat?) comes back to Earth, he has only aged a few years, but his brother has died of old age. It's a very poignant book, as 1950s juvenile pulp sci-fi goes.

Anyway. Back to software. (Aw, do we have to talk about *that* again? I was enjoying that brief digression into space travel.) When you write software, you have to deal with so much time dilation that science fiction sounds positively *normal*.

Days Are Seconds

It usually takes days of design, programming, and testing to create a fragment of software that a user will experience in a matter of seconds. For commercial-quality software, a typical small dialog box might take about four days to code, realistically. But the user will only spend ten seconds in that dialog box.

What that means is that some aspects of the dialog may make *perfect* sense to you as a programmer, because you spent four days thinking about them, but they won't necessarily make sense to a user, who has to figure them out in a couple of seconds.

Figure 14-1, taken from Corel PHOTO-PAINT 9, shows one tab of a print dialog that probably took months to design and create. The attention to detail shows throughout: there's a handy preview pane, which graphically illustrates what the rest of the dialog means.

However, there are still a lot of things here which probably made perfect sense to the programmer after three months of thinking about printing, but which users will probably not figure out so quickly. What's all that stuff about tiling? What's an *imposition layout*? The fact that the programmer had so much time to learn about printing while the user has only a couple of minutes, at most, leads to a real imbalance of power. The programmer is *convinced* that the dialog is quite straight-forward and easy to use, and the user is just downright flummoxed. *Flummoxed!*

The best solution to the "Days = Seconds" time warp is to do hall-way usability tests. After designing your dialog, print it out, take it down the hall to the lunchroom, and ask the first three people you see to explain the dialog to you. If there are any serious problems, this will probably uncover them.

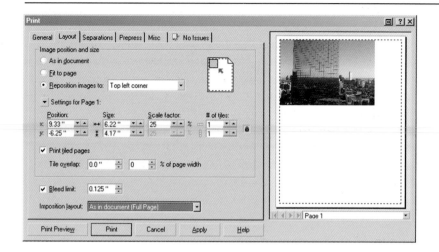

FIGURE 14-1

This tabbed Print dialog probably took months of work. But most users will not be willing to spend more than about ten seconds figuring out how to print.

Months Are Minutes

Let's pretend, for the sake of argument, that you discover that there's a real, unmet need for grilled marshmallows in the workplace. "Popcorn and Cappuccinos are *passé*," you think. So you set out to create a marshmallow-grilling device that you hope will take the world by storm.

At first, your concept is quite simple. There's a slot in the top into which you pop the marshmallows. Seconds later, they emerge, fully grilled and toasty warm, from a tray on the bottom, ready to be eaten.

While you are trying to explain the whole concept to a manufacturer of business-grade heating elements, the guy erupts in laughter. "Grilled marshmallows? Without *graham crackers?* Who would eat one of those things without graham crackers?" Now you start to worry. Most of the people you talked to seemed to like the idea, and many of them explicitly stated that they *hate* graham crackers, but a bit more research shows that there's a whole population of people that just will not eat their grilled marshmallows unless they have graham crackers. So you add a *second* slot to your design, for graham crackers.

As time goes on, more problems are discovered. Certain inferior brands of marshmallows cannot be reliably grilled without catching fire, so you add a little fire extinguisher button on the front panel that puts out any accidental fires. The CEO you hired points out that you're now two thirds of the way to making s'mores, so you add a third slot for putting in chocolate bars, and a S'more button, which makes a tasty chocolate, marshmallow, and graham cracker sandwich (although graham crackers come in two sizes, so you have to add a switch to choose the size).

Then usability testing reveals that some people like their marshmallows almost raw, while others want them virtually *charred* with liquefied middles (mmmm). It's not just a matter of how long they cook: it's a matter of how quickly you turn them over the heat, whether the heat is radiant or from a flame, and so on. Eventually your little marshmallow-grilling device has six different adjustment knobs and two kinds of heating elements.

"This is for the workplace," your head UI designer tells you. "It will be used by many different people. Those people aren't going to want to remember all their personal settings." So you add a Save Settings button with a little LCD panel, and a Load Settings button. Now, you can file your personal marshmallow-grilling settings under your own name.

"Privacy!" scream the privacy advocates. "What if we want to be able to save our settings *without* every gossip in the office knowing how we like our s'mores?!" Fine. A password feature is added.

"What if someone forgets their password?" Now it's getting ridiculous. OK. The password feature is enhanced with one of those silly challenge-response questions like "What's your mother's maiden name?" and, if hooked up to the LAN, it can email you your password when you forget it.

By now, the tiny LCD panel has grown into a 15" color screen, the control panel looks like the cockpit of the space shuttle, and it costs $1275 to manufacture. But after two years in development, the thing finally ships!

Your very first customer buys one and takes it home, excited. But when she gets it out of the box, there's a two-hundred-page manual, a software license agreement, a control panel with dozens of buttons, a programming handbook for the scripting language, and the screen is asking her if she wants to sign up for AOL.

The "Months = Minutes" rule is a corollary to the "Days = Seconds" rule. When you create a new software package, even a fairly simple one, it typically takes between six months and two years from the initial conception to shipping the final bits. During those months or years, you have an *awful* lot of time to learn about your own program and how it works. When you invent a new concept every month or so for two years, the learning curve is not very steep—for you. For your user, it means there are twelve things to learn right out of the box in the first five minutes of using the dang thing.

The products that we recognize as being the *best* designs always seem to have the fewest buttons. While those products were being created, it's pretty obvious that the designers kept thinking of ways to *simplify* the interface, not complicate it. Eventually VCR designers realized that when you stick a videotape in the slot, they should switch from TV to VCR mode and start, um, *playing the tape*. And then they figured out that when it's done playing the tape, it might as well rewind and eject it. For watching movies, at least, you don't need to press a single button.

As you design and build your product, try to notice if you are *adding* complications or *removing* complications. If you're adding complications, remember that something that seems easy when you have months to design it is not going to seem so easy when your user has only minutes to learn about it.

Seconds Are Hours

The third time warp rule is that it doesn't take very long before somebody gets bored and decides that your program is slow. If your program feels slow, your users won't feel in control, and they'll be less happy. "Seconds = Hours" refers to the fact that if you make somebody wait, say, nine seconds, they will whine and cry about how it took *hours*. People are not very fair. You can give them a Web site where they can find over thirty-four thousand recipes for tuna casserole in seconds, something that used to take a trip to Washington, D.C. and *months* of research in the *Ladies Home Journal* archives of the Library of Congress, but if a recipe takes thirty seconds to appear on the screen, your ingrate users will moan about the "World Wide Wait" and how slow their modem is.

How long is too long? This has been the subject of *years* of debate among usability experts and Human Boredom Research scientists. I am happy to announce that after an exhaustive survey of over twenty thousand college sophomores, I have the final answer. Boredom kicks in after 2.73 seconds, precisely. So let's all keep our latency to 2.72 seconds or less, OK?

Just kidding!

The real answer is that it's not the passage of time that's boring, it's boredom that's boring. I can walk three miles down Fifth Avenue in Manhattan without getting bored, but walking a thousand feet past featureless cow pasture in Kansas feels like it takes an eternity. Boredom is a function of the rate at which stimulating things happen to your brain.

When someone clicks on a link on a Web site, they are probably not doing anything but waiting for that page to appear. So if it takes ten seconds to show up instead of five seconds, it seems like a really long time. On the other hand, when they start to download the latest Ricky Martin MP3 over a modem, it's going to take twenty minutes, so they find something else to do while they wait. And if it takes twenty-one minutes instead of twenty minutes, it's no big deal.

To fight boredom, create the *illusion* of low latency. Good UI designers use three tricks to do this.

Trick One. Always respond *immediately* to the user's request, even if you don't have a final answer. There's nothing more annoying than a program that appears as if it's not responding to mouse clicks simply because it's performing a long operation. You should always give an immediate response, even if it's nothing more than changing the cursor to an hourglass or displaying a progress indicator. (Among other things, this lets the user know that the program received their click. A program that doesn't respond immediately to mouse and keyboard input appears dead to the user. At the very least, they will click again.)

Trick Two. Find creative ways to break up long operations. The best example I've seen of this is in Microsoft Visual Basic. The designers of the Basic compiler realized that almost all of the time spent compiling is actually spent parsing the program text (that is, breaking down a line of code into its constituent parts). If it takes, say, half a second to parse a single line of code, and one one-hundredth of a second for everything else, then a hundred-line program will take fifty-one seconds to compile. But the Visual Basic designers put the parser into the *editor*. When you hit `Enter` after typing a line of text into the editor, that line is immediately parsed and stored in parsed form. So now, hitting `Enter` takes half a second, barely perceptible, and compiling a hundred-line program takes one second, also barely perceptible.

Trick Three is the exact *opposite* of Trick Two. When all else fails, *bunch together* all the slow operations. The classic example is your extremely slow setup program. It's slow because it has to download files, uncompress them, and install them. There's nothing you can do about that. But what you *can* do is make sure that all the slow bits are done at the end, *after* gathering any required input from the user. Have you ever started a long installation procedure and gone to watch TV, only to come back an hour later to find that the setup program has stopped and is waiting for you to OK the license agreement before it starts downloading? When you have a really long operation, always get *all* the input you need from the user first, then tell them explicitly that "this will take a while. Go get some M&Ms."

CHAPTER

15

"But...How Do It Know?"

Remember the old advertising slogan for Thermoses? They "Keep Hot Drinks Hot and Cold Drinks Cold!" To which your slightly brighter-than-average five-year-old asks: "But...how do it *know?*"

That's what we in the software design field call a *heuristic*. Here are a few well-known examples of heuristics:

- If you type the word "teh" in Microsoft Word, Word will decide you probably meant "the" and change it for you.

- If you enter "Monday" into a cell in Microsoft Excel and then drag down, you get the days of the week (see Figure 15-1).

- When you search for text that looks like an address using the Google search engine, it will offer to show you a map of that location.

- If you buy a lot of Danielle Steel books on Amazon.com, and a new one comes out, the next time you visit Amazon.com they will try to sell it to you.

As a rule of thumb, the way you know something is a heuristic is that it makes you wonder, "how do it know?" The term *heuristic* itself comes from the field of artificial intelligence, where it's used when the

FIGURE 15-1

Excel has heuristically decided that you must want the days of the week because you happened to type Monday. (But... how do it know?)

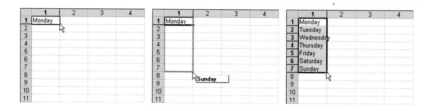

fuzziness of real life doesn't line up properly with the sharp true/false world of computers. A more formal definition is that a heuristic is a rule that's *probably* right, but not guaranteed to be right:

- English speakers intend to type "the" much more often than they intend to type "teh." If they typed "teh," it's probably a mistake.

- When you type "Monday," you are probably referring to the day of the week. If you expand out the series, you probably want to see days of the week.

- When you type something that looks like a number followed by a name followed by the word "Street," it's probably an address.

- If you buy a lot of Danielle Steel books on Amazon.com, you'll probably want to buy the new one.

The operative word here is always *probably*. We're not sure. That's why it's just a heuristic, not a hard and fast *rule*.

In the olden days of programming, heuristics were very, very uncommon, because programmers are very logical creatures and they don't like rules that are "98% right." In the logical world of programmers, "teh" and "the" are equally valid sequences of three ASCII characters, and there is no logical reason to give one of them special treatment. But as soon as the designers of Microsoft Word broke through this mental logjam, they realized that there were zillions of interesting *assumptions* you could make about what people wanted. If you typed a paragraph starting with an asterisk, you probably want a bullet! If you type a bunch of hyphens, you probably want a horizontal line! If you start out a document with "Dear Mom," you're probably writing her a letter!

In their zeal for heuristics, the designers of Microsoft Office came up with more and more clever features, which they marketed as IntelliSense. As a marketing pitch, these features sound really neat. Word *figures out* what you want and does it "automatically!"

Unfortunately, somewhere, something went wrong. Woody Leonhard wrote a whole book called *Word 97 Annoyances*, mostly about how to turn off the various heuristics, and people were so thankful they gave the book five-star ratings on Amazon.com. Somehow, heuristics crossed the line from "doing what you want automatically" to "annoyances."

Nobody sets out to write annoying software. So where *is* the line? When does a heuristic stop being a really cool, helpful feature that saves time and start being an annoyance?

Here's the thought process that goes into developing a typical heuristic:

1. If the user types "teh," there's a 99% chance they meant "the."

2. So we'll just change it to "the" for them. Then there's a 1% chance that we're wrong.

3. If we're wrong, the user will have to undo the change we made.

4. Ninety-nine out of one hundred times, we improved the user's life. One time out of one hundred, we made it worse. Net value to user: 98% improvement.

This tends to get generalized as:

1. If the user does x, there's an n% chance they meant y.

2. So we'll just do y for them. Then there's a $(100 - n)$ chance that we're wrong.

3. If we're wrong, the user will have to correct us.

4. Net value to user: $(100 - 2n)$%, which is better than doing nothing for $n > 50$.

Aha! I think I've found the bug. It's in step 4, which does *not* logically follow. Happiness is not linear. It doesn't really make a user *that* happy when they type "teh" and get "the." And happiness is not cumulative. The bottom line is that every single time you apply a heuristic *incorrectly,* you are making the user *a lot more unhappy* than you made them happy by applying the heuristic correctly all the other times. Annoyances are annoyances, and people don't weigh annoyances against joy when deciding how happy to be. They just get annoyed.

How annoyed? That depends on step 3: how hard it is to *undo* the heuristic if the program guessed wrong. In Word, it's supposed to be pretty easy: you can just hit Ctrl+Z, which means Undo. But a lot of people, even people who know about the Undo command, don't realize that Undo undoes the *computer's* actions as well as their own. And if you watch them, they usually try to undo the error themselves by backspacing and retyping, and of course, Word blindly applies the wrong heuristic *again*, and now they're getting *really* frustrated and they don't know how to fix it. By now the annoyance factor is deep into the triple digits, which has more than wiped out the minor satisfaction that the heuristic was intended to cause in the first place.

In general, I don't like heuristics because of the principle from Chapter 2:

If your program model is nontrivial, it's probably not the same as the user model.

This gets back to the "How Do It Know" factor. If users can't figure out *why* the program is applying a heuristic, they will certainly be surprised by it, producing a classic example of "the user model doesn't correspond to the (inscrutable) program model," and therefore, the program will be hard to use. To judge a heuristic, you have to decide if the rule for the heuristic is obvious enough, or if users are going to stare blankly at the screen and say, "how do it know?" Turning "teh" into "the" may be obvious, but changing three dashes into a horizontal line is probably *not* what people expected, and they probably won't know why it's happening. This makes it a bad heuristic because it leads people to say, "how do it know?"

The second way to judge a heuristic is by the difficulty of undoing it, and how obvious the undo procedure is. When you write a check in Intuit's Quicken program, and you start typing the name of the payee, Quicken looks for other payees that start with the same letters as the payee you're typing and pretypes that for you. So if you've paid someone named "Lucian the Meatball" in the past, and you type "Lu," Quicken will propose the full name "Lucian the Meatball." That's the heuristic part, and it's pretty obvious why it's happening—nobody's going to ask "how do it know?" But the brilliant part of Quicken is that the "cian the Meatball" part will be selected, so that if the heuristic was wrong, all you have to do was keep typing and it will effectively undo the heuristic right away. (This invention spread from Intuit's Quicken to Microsoft Excel and eventually to Microsoft Windows). When a heuristic is really easy to undo, and it's obvious how to undo it, people won't be so annoyed.

The third way to judge a heuristic is, of course, by how likely it is to be correct. Changing "teh" to "the" is pretty likely to be correct (although it was wrong about ten times while I was typing this chapter). But a lot of other heuristics are less likely to be correct (such as Word's morbid insistence that I want help writing a letter).

> *A good heuristic is obvious, easily undone, and extremely likely to be correct. Other heuristics are annoying.*

CHAPTER

16

Tricks of the Trade

Here we are, almost at the end of the book, and I still have a whole bunch of important factoids to tell you that don't fit neatly into chapters. But they're pretty important factoids:

- Know how to use color.

- Know how to use icons.

- Know the rules of internationalization.

Let's go through these one at a time.

Know How to Use Color

When I set up my office files, I bought a big box of file folders. The box came with four different color folders: red, yellow, manila, and blue. I decided to use one color for clients, one color for employees, one color for receipts, and the fourth color for everything else. Outrageously sensible, right?

No. The truth is that when I'm not looking at the files, I can't remember the color scheme, and in fact, the color scheme doesn't seem to help at all. As it turns out, using different colors is good for *distinguishing* things, but not for *coding* things. If you have a bunch of red folders and a bunch of blue folders, it's easy to tell that they are different, but it's harder to remember which color means which.

The general rule for how to use color was best stated by Web designer Diane Wilson:

> ### *"Design in black and white. Add color for emphasis, when your design is complete."*

Strange as it may seem, creating a color code doesn't really work. People have trouble remembering the association of colors to meanings. In fact, if you make a pie chart using five different colors, with a little legend showing the meaning of the colors, it's surprising how hard it is cognitively for people to figure out which wedge belongs to which label. It's not impossible, of course, it's just not super easy. Putting labels next to the wedges is a million times easier (see Figure 16-1).

FIGURE 16-1

People have trouble remembering color codes. Don't rely on color to convey meaning.

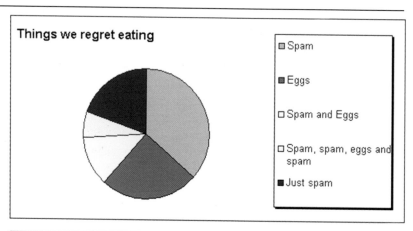

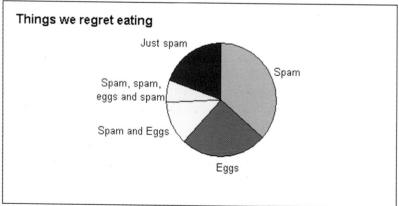

There's another important reason you can't rely on color to convey meaning: many people can't see it. No, I don't mean the old timers who still have green-on-green screens. But about 5% of all males (and a much smaller number of females) have some degree of color blindness and simply cannot distinguish colors (particularly red and green, which is why stoplights are vertical).

Color can be used successfully for a few things:

1. As decoration—in pictures, icons, and text, where the effect is solely decorative.

2. To separate things—as long as you do not rely on the color as the only indicator, you can use color as one distinguishing factor, for example, by using a different color and a larger font for headings.

3. To indicate availability—by using grey to indicate an option that isn't available. Even most colorblind users can distinguish greys from blacks. Similarly you can use lightly shaded backgrounds to indicate areas where the user can't edit, and white backgrounds to indicate areas where the user can edit. This has been a GUI convention for so long that most people understand it subconsciously.

Always honor the system color settings, that is, the colors that the user chose in the control panel. Users have deliberately chosen those colors to give their computer the color scheme they like. Also, many of your vision-impaired users have deliberately set up schemes that they can see more clearly. (For that matter, always honor the system fonts so that your text is readable by people who prefer larger fonts.)

Know How to Use Icons

A picture is worth a thousand words, you think? Well, not if you're trying to make a picture of the "schedule meeting" command and you've only got 256 pixels total to do it in. (I know, I know, now you're all going to email me your clever icon renditions of "schedule meeting" in 256 pixels...) Here's the trick with icons. As a rule of thumb, they work pretty well for *nouns*, especially real-world objects, where you can create an icon by making a picture of the thing. But they don't work so well for verbs, because 16 ×16 is not a lot of space to show an action. In a typical word processor, the icon for numbered lists (Figure 16-2) is amazingly obvious. Hey, it looks like a numbered list! But the icon for "Paste" (Figure 16-3) is not so obvious. Even after you've learned it, it requires too much cognitive effort to recall.

FIGURE 16-2

The icon for numbered lists is just a picture of what it does, so it's easy to recognize.

FIGURE 16-3

The icon for Paste is attempting to depict a verb, so it's not very easy to recognize.

Know the Rules of Internationalization

You may not be internationalizing your product now, but chances are, you will. The cost of translating a software product is far less than the cost of writing it in the first place, and you can often sell as many copies in a second language as you can in the original (especially if the original language is Icelandic, and you're translating it to English.) There are a lot of rules about how to write good international software, which are beyond the scope of this book. In fact, there are whole books on the topic. But for user interface design, there are three crucial things you should try to keep in mind.

Rule One: the translated text is almost always longer than the original. Sometimes it's because some languages like to use forty-seven-letter words for the *simplest* concepts. (Ahem! You know who you are!) Sometimes it's just because when you translate something, you need more words to convey the exact meaning of the word in the original language. In any case, if your user interface relies on certain important words fitting into a certain number of pixels, you're almost always going to have trouble when you go to translate it.

Rule Two: think about cultural variables. Americans should realize that phone numbers are not always seven digits long with a dash after the third digit. If somebody's name is X Y, don't assume that they are Mr. Y; they could just as well be Mrs. X. Non-Americans should remember that Americans don't have the foggiest idea what a centimeter is (they think it's a multilegged creepy-crawly). Microsoft Excel uses a U.S. dollar sign icon ($) to format cells as currency, but in non-U.S. versions of Excel, they use an icon showing coins instead. And don't get me started about lexical sort orders or the odd way the Swedes sort things—you could never find yourself in the phone book in Stockholm, even if you lived there and had a Swedish telephone, and so forth.

Rule Three: be culturally sensitive. If your software shows maps, even for something innocuous like time-zone selection, be *real* careful about where the borders go, because somewhere, someone is going to get offended. (Microsoft now has a full-time employee who worries about this, after Windows 95 was banned in India for failing to reflect India's claim on Kashmir—a matter of a few pixels in the time-zone control panel.)

Don't use a little pig for your "Save" icon (get it? Piggy banks? Savings?) because piggy banks aren't universal. In fact, don't use puns anywhere in your user interface (or in your speeches, or books, or even in your private journal; they are *not funny*). Don't use a hand palm-up to mean "stop," because it's offensive in some cultures.

In general, don't release software in another language without doing a little bit of cultural testing on native speakers. I had a scanner once that displayed a dialog box saying, and I quote: "The Scanner begins to warm up!" The upper case 'S' in "scanner" was proof, but the whole sentence just *sounds* like it was written in German and translated to English (as, indeed, it was). Weird, huh? There's nothing grammatically wrong with it, but it doesn't sound like something a native English speaker would say. One famous program from Australia, Trumpet Winsock, made Americans think that it was written by an illiterate moron, mainly because it used the word "Dialler" all over the user interface, which Americans spell, "Dialer." To an American, using two 'L's looks like the kind of mistake a young child might make. (Other Australian spellings, like "neighbour," look merely British to the average American, not illiterate).

The best way to become culturally sensitive, I think, is to live in another country for a year or two, and travel extensively. It's especially helpful if that country has nice warm beaches, or wonderful cultural institutions, or spectacularly beautiful people. Great restaurants also help. You should ask your boss to pay for this as a part of your UI training. And when you've figured out where the best beaches and restaurants are, you should top off your training with a course in UI design from someone like, ahem, myself.

17

Designing for the Web

The Web is an incredibly diverse medium. It's impossible to provide hard-and-fast rules that apply equally to a toy store, a movie site, a newspaper, a graphic designer's portfolio, a teenager's journal, and the IBM full-text database of all patents issued since 1971. Many of the books about Web usability seem to assume you're making a corporate site or an e-commerce site. So they are full of rules like "Flash is Bad!" which are just too single-minded to possibly be correct for the wide variety of Web sites out there.

All the principles I've talked about up until now are just as important when you're designing Web sites. Your Web site will be usable if the user model matches the program model. For example, almost every Web site has a little logo in the top left corner, and when you click it, it almost always takes you to the home page. This is so common that people have come to expect it. That's the user model. If your Web site has a logo in the top left corner, and clicking on the logo doesn't do anything, people are going to have trouble using your site. The user model says that things that are blue and underlined are links. If your graphic designers think that underlines look ugly, and they don't underline the links on your site, people won't click. Bonk.

But there are two specific problems you have to watch out for when you design for the Web: time delay and the limitations of HTML.

On the Web, Nobody Knows You're on the Moon

One of the biggest restrictions in designing for the Web is another time-travel problem like the ones discussed in Chapter 14. On the Web, the problem is *time delay*, also known as *lag*. When you talk to a user through the Web, it takes them a long time to hear you. Several things conspire to create the slow response time of the Web: slow modem speeds, slow servers, and general Internet latency. Really, really fast pages under optimal conditions might load in a couple of seconds, but in many cases, pages can take fifteen seconds to a minute (or even more) to appear. Your users, for all intents and purposes, are on the moon.

Think of a Web application like, for example, the New York Times. You've got a page with a bunch of headlines. When you click on a headline, a new page loads where you can read the entire story. If reading each story takes ninety seconds, and pages take ten seconds to appear, you are spending 90% of your time reading, which is pretty decent.

In an effort to move up in the Web ratings, the *New York Times* recently started splitting up each article into two or more Web pages. Hmmm. Now we're spending around 80% of our time reading, which is a little bit less usable.

But wait, it can get worse. As soon as you're developing an *application* for the Web, as opposed to merely a newspaper or content-based site, things get really clunky. HTML was designed for simple interactions. "Show me this page. Now show me that page. Oops. That's not what I meant, take me back to where I was before." As soon as the interactions get more complicated, HTML starts to look like pretty thin soup. Here's an example.

iPrint.com is a pretty neat service that I've been using to print the business cards for my consulting company. You can design your business cards over the Web, and when you're done, they print them and mail them to you. Using the iPrint.com interactive designer, you can add text, move things around, change fonts, add logos, and so forth. Every time you try to do something like move the logo a smidgen to the left, it requires a round-trip to the Web server, which, today, is taking me about half a minute. As you edit the business card, you spend about two seconds thinking about what to do next, and then half a minute waiting for the result, which means you spend more than 90% of your time waiting. This can get kind of frustrating. It's *especially* frustrating when you're trying to "tweak" the sizes and positions of objects (see Figure 17-1). Don't get me wrong; the designers of

FIGURE 17-1

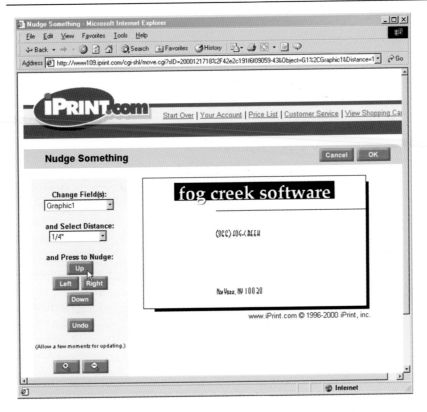

iPrint.com have done a heroic job of trying to work within the limitations of HTML, but designing business cards this way is just too dang painful compared to using, say, a thirteen-year-old copy of MacPaint.

Web interfaces that make you spend so much time waiting just feel *clunky*, like an old one-speed bicycle with some teeth missing from the gear. At an emotional level, when you get results immediately, you are happy because you feel like you're in control. When you have to wait, you become unhappy. If you have to wait twenty-three times to make a business card, the unhappiness will start to accrue.

A better technology for creating complicated UIs like this might be to use Dynamic HTML or Java Applets. At the very least, your users can lay things out on the screen using a point-and-click interface that responds immediately. Many Web designers have given up on Java Applets for mission-critical work because of the long downloads, the compatibility problems that make it "write once, debug everywhere," and the fact that Java UIs look kind of weird, they don't match the operating system UI exactly. Dynamic HTML has even worse compatibility problems. This is one of those hard trade-offs you always have to make as a designer. Sigh.

Here's another example of the time delay problem: email software. A common activity in managing your email is deleting messages. Some days, all I really have time to do is delete messages. Every couple of weeks, 7,326 messages have accumulated in my inbox, and I need to prune away, at the very least, the stupidest of the jokes that were forwarded to me and the "opportunities" to erase credit card debt or unsightly blemishes.

With a Windows email program like Eudora or Outlook, selecting a message and deleting it can be done virtually instantaneously. Click the mouse, press the Del key, all done! So picking 34 messages from your inbox and deleting them all is quite easy and not unpleasant. (Except on those odd occasions when certain email programs, for some inexplicable reason, decide to *potchke* around reindexing their files, so the delete operation takes six hours and displays a progress indicator. But that's rare.)

When you're using a Web-based email system like Hotmail, that message about Microsoft buying Norway is stored away on a server. So when you delete it, a message has to be sent to the Web server, which is probably pretty busy delivering spam to a few million people. Eventually the server gets around to processing your request and deleting the message, but then the server has to requery the database to see what messages you still have left in your inbox, construct a new HTML page with the shorter list, stick a flashing-monkeys ad on the top, and send it all back to you over the Internet and a modem that's advertised as 56K but which really never really connects any faster than 43K (those *crooks!*).

Anyhow, the end result is that a single delete operation takes thirty seconds of user time, not zero seconds. It wouldn't be the end of the world if you were just deleting one message. But we're deleting 34 messages, remember? Which now *theoretically* takes seventeen minutes, but it probably takes a lot longer, because while you were waiting for the fourth message to be deleted, the cat jumped up on your desk and spilled a cup of hot tea and ran away in fright, and now you have to decide whether to chase the cat and mollify her, or get some paper towels to wipe up the tea before it ruins *another* keyboard. Frustrating, huh?

Most designers of email-on-the-Web interfaces are aware of this time lag, and they've compensated for it by putting little checkboxes next to each message (see Figure 17-2). You can check off a bunch of messages and delete them all at once. That's a pretty good way to

FIGURE 17-2

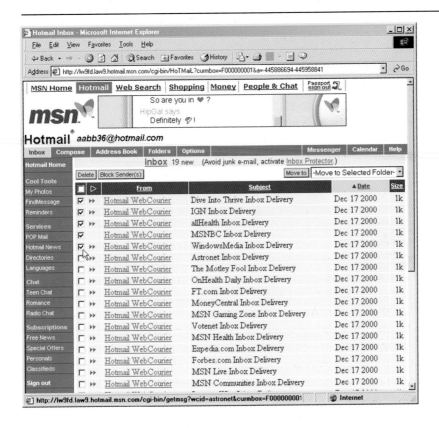

A good example of reducing round-trips: Web-based email providers usually give you little checkboxes so you can delete a bunch of messages with one round-trip to the server.

reduce frustration. Although it's not the most intuitive thing in the world, it sure is better than nothing. We're working in a difficult medium here, and we'll take anything we can get. In general, a good rule for Web services is:

> *On the Web, every click results in a round-trip to the server, which reduces usability. Design to minimize round-trips.*

Another example of this rule can be seen in Web discussion sites. There are lots of different interfaces for discussion groups on the Web, but they basically fall into two categories: the type of interface that shows you one message per page (like *The Motley Fool* or *Yahoo! Finance*), and the type of interface that shows you a whole bunch of messages all on one page (like Slashdot.org, famous for its highly usable, if not learnable, discussion interface).

If you were actually reading up until now, as opposed to daydreaming about something more interesting like Ultimate Frisbee, you should be able to figure out which one I think is better. Even though *Yahoo!* has a super fast Web server, when you try to read discussions on *Yahoo!*, you spend a lot of time waiting for the next message to arrive and then getting frustrated when it turns out to be moronic. But when you try to read discussions on *Slashdot*, all you have to do is scroll down through a long Web page; it's much more fluid, there is no waiting, and you can skip over morons as fast as you can move your eyeball. Within a few minutes you know that *everything* posted up there is moronic and you can just go play Ultimate Frisbee before it gets dark.

The single-page discussion UI probably exists because those sites are supported by ads, and the more pages you look at, the more ads they can try to show you. Not that you'll care. If you're actually following a discussion, you are not going to look at the ads. If you track the pupils of someone following a discussion, I'll bet that they never *once* look anywhere *near* the ad banner as they flip from message to message in the discussion group. The banner could contain a row of flashing orange naked monkeys offering you fifty thousand dollars in actual United States cash if you would just *click here*, but nobody would notice. It doesn't matter, because those sites get paid for every ad they show you, and they are generally happy to ruin their user interfaces if it means a few more advertiser dollars.

HTML Is Not a Windowing System

The next big limitation of the Web is that Web pages just can't do everything that you can do with a modern, state-of-the-art windowing system, or even with an utterly obsolete windowing system, say, the original Macintosh from 1984. There are just too many things that you can't do.

Menus are one example. Suppose you have a Web site which serves customers in several countries. On the home page, you would like to have a link to the specific site for each country where you do business. For a large company, that could be eighty countries. There's just not enough room to have a link to each of them.

Well, you could have a link on the home page that says "Worldwide Sites," which goes to another page with links for every country. This requires two clicks just to get into the site, which is going to cost you a lot of visitors who just get fed up and click away to AmIHotOrNot.com to look at cuties.

A more common approach is to try to create a dropdown menu. A dropdown menu is the Murphy Bed of GUIs. It's a real-estate gimmick to fit a lot of stuff into a little space. Unfortunately, HTML doesn't *have* dropdown menus. The feature just doesn't exist.

There are two common ways Web designers try to work around the lack of menus.

The first is by constructing some kind of JavaScript/Dynamic HTML menu-like thing. That works OK, but it's not terrific, because not all Web browsers support JavaScript and Dynamic HTML, and when they do, the implementations are usually buggy enough that every incremental release of every browser is likely to break your script. Not only that, but when you are done, your carefully created menu probably does not work in exactly the same way as a regular menu. The dropdown menus on Microsoft's current home page are really more like fall-down menus that plop down if you even move your mouse over them. In Windows itself, the menus won't drop down unless you click on them. The lack of consistency, as I have hopefully drilled into you by now, can create usability problems.

A slightly easier way to provide menus in a Web page is by using a dropdown listbox, which sort of looks like it might be a menu, but, um, no, it's not a menu. It is visually different (see Figure 17-3). It doesn't behave like a menu. In GUI apps, there has been a long-standing rule that changing an item on a dropdown should *not* take any major action like navigating. It is only supposed to be used to change a setting. You still have to press an OK button to take the action. One good reason that this rule exists is that dropdown listboxes require a lot of mouse-dexterity (see Chapter 10), and as you know, people can't use the mouse.

FIGURE 17-3

Choose your country:

United States ▼
United States
Asia-Pacific region
Brazil
Canada
Germany
Mexico
Sweden
United Kingdom

Using dropdown listboxes for menus is inconsistent and confusing.

Many clever Web designers have realized that by using JavaScript, you can detect when the user has changed the contents of the dropdown. So they make a dropdown which actually navigates for you as soon as you choose something. This is almost always a bad UI. When the user makes a mistake and selects the wrong item, which is quite common, they will find themselves navigated to a new page. And they will be surprised by this, too, because the GUI convention for dropdown listboxes is that they *don't take any action*. Whenever you surprise people, you are *by definition* making a bad UI choice. If the user lets go of the mouse button on the wrong choice and the page flips right away, they will have to back up and start over. Frustrating.

Another thing that's really hard to do well in HTML is make a dialog box. Some designers have attempted to simulate dialog boxes by popping up a secondary window. But that's not *quite* good enough. The secondary window is not a child window of the main browser window, so it doesn't stay on top. If you click back on the main window, the secondary window gets covered up. And the secondary window must load its contents from the Web, which is going to take some time. By now, many people have come to associate secondary windows with ads. Many people will just automatically hit the close box before they even realize you're showing them a dialog box, not an ad. (Leave it to advertisers to spoil it for the rest of us.) Yet again, the limitations of HTML foil our attempts to use common GUI metaphors.

The closest thing you can do to make a dialog box is simply to navigate to another page with a form on it. That's not quite as good as a real live dialog box. Why? Well, a dialog box pops up on a window *above* your work, which is a real-world metaphor that gives people confidence that their original work hasn't gone away, it has merely been *interrupted*. Without overlapping windows, people lose their bearings and forget where they are and how they got there. But for now, it will have to do.

Yet another thing you can't do on the Web is provide a decent text-editing widget. The best you can do is put up a big TEXTAREA, which is about as user-friendly as Windows' *Notepad* without the Save command. When you're composing a really long email to your Aunt Marge with Hotmail, there's no way to save your work regularly. So if you accidentally close the Web browser, the entire three-page story about how the neighbor's ferret got into your grape pie is just *lost*. This doesn't happen with regular email programs which have a *Save* command and which don't let you close windows without prompting you to save.

Use the Web Browser's UI

Let's think for a minute about what makes a Web browser so easy to use in the first place. It only has a three interface features you need to learn about to be productive:

1. Clicking on a link

2. Scrolling

3. Clicking on the Back button (optional)

A very distant fourth is filling out forms, so you can order Harry Potter books from Amazon.com. Almost everything else in the UI is fluff. That's why Web browsers are so easy to use.

Historical Note

Some early Web usability gurus did some usability tests and discovered that people don't know how to scroll. What they failed to notice was how quickly people *learn* this skill. Once again, they confused usability with learnability. In the meantime, an uncanny amount of damage has been done by Web site designers who try to cram their sites into a tiny rectangle so that their site is viewable without scrolling, usually by using a font so small most people have to strain to read it. Luckily, the "nobody knows how to scroll" superstition is wearing off.

One assumption we've been making all along is that when you make a Web site, you have to design a UI for it. But the interesting thing is that almost anything you can do to *avoid* designing a UI is probably going to *improve* the usability of your site. If you rely on links instead of making a funny dropdown navigator, all the people whose brains are only just large enough to remember those three primary interface features will still be able to use your site.

One thing sort of amusing about this is that it seems to be a general rule that the fewer nifty features you use, the more usable your site will be, because people have already figured out the default Web browser UI:

- If you don't change the color used to display links, the Web browser's defaults will apply. These defaults provide a different color for visited and unvisited links. So, people will be able to see at a glance which parts of your site they've visited, making it easier to scan through and avoid reading things twice.

- If you don't use GIF images for buttons, but just use buttons instead, your buttons will look the same as all the other buttons on the Web and people will realize that they can push them.

- If you don't use funny redirects, you won't break the Back button on Web browsers and people will be able to back out of your site.

- If you don't use Flash or Shockwave for your content, Web search engines will be able to index your site, so people searching for your site will find it. If you use a cool Flash animation for all your press releases, your press releases will not be available to search engines and fewer people will find them.

- If you don't use frames, people will be able to create shortcuts to any page on your site. They will be able to cut and paste the URL from the address bar into an email message. If you use frames, the address bar doesn't necessarily change to reflect the current frame contents.

These are just a few examples of how limiting yourself to the most basic features of HTML can make Web sites more usable. Basically, the Web evolved a little too quickly. All the neat features that were added since the earliest versions of HTML weren't really deeply integrated into the structure of the Web, so today they are not universally available and they are not universally understood. Flash and Java applets are some of the worst offenders, because they create a rectangle of lawlessness, inside of which every designer has to reinvent the user interface from the ground up, something which is rarely done in a consistent way.

Bottom line:

The fewer cool Web features you use, the more usable your site will be.

Please don't let this stop you if you are making a site that's meant to be entertaining rather than useful. *Usability is not everything.* If usability engineers designed a nightclub, it would be clean, quiet, brightly lit, with lots of places to sit down, plenty of bartenders, menus written in 18-point sans serif, and easy-to-find bathrooms. But nobody would be there. They would all be down the street at Coyote Ugly pouring beer on each other.

CHAPTER

18

Programming for Humans

My sense of user sympathy as a moral imperative (rather than just a way to sell more software) started when I heard a story from an Excel usability test. A woman came in to test the software. When she wasn't able to complete the assigned task, she actually *broke down in tears*. Ken Dye, the usability lab manager, told me he had to walk her around the idyllic Microsoft campus until she felt better. After that, we were always very careful to explain to usability participants that we were testing *the product*, not their performance, and we *expected* that they wouldn't be able to accomplish some tasks. Not that that helped. People feel *miserable* when they can't accomplish a task.

I was reminded of a story about the task list in Microsoft Outlook. In the original design, when you completed a task, it was simply deleted from the list. Logical. But the designers discovered that people had more of a sense of accomplishment if they could actually cross the items off the list, and this made them happier. So now, when you mark a task as completed, Outlook draws a line through it rather than making it disappear completely (see Figure 18-1).

Mahatma Gandhi considered it violence against nature to throw away even the stub of a pencil because it wasted the world's resources. And he considered it violence against humanity, too, because our

CHAPTER 18

FIGURE 18-1

The Outlook task list actually crosses off items as you complete them, simply because it made people happier.

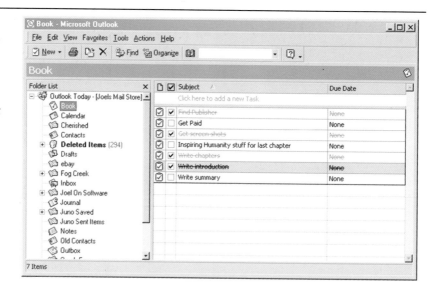

over-consumption denies resources to people who live in poverty. The Talmud was concerned about even tiny acts of waste: as little as a mustard seed, which was considered the smallest thing the human eye could see. Even passing a glass of water over a loaf of bread at the dinner table was forbidden, because if the water spilled, the bread would be ruined. What they're both teaching us is that small things matter; that everyone has opportunities all the time to improve the world in a tiny way, to show respect for all living things.

Usability, fundamentally, is a matter of bringing a bit of human rights into the world of computer-human interaction. It's a way to let our ideals shine through in our software, no matter how mundane the software is. You may think that you're stuck in a boring, drab IT department making mind-numbing inventory software that only five lonely people will ever use. But you have daily opportunities to show respect for humanity even with the most mundane software. Even if you are just working on a code library, an API that is invisible to everyone but other programmers, if you can design the API in a way that is consistent, easily understood, more obvious, and easier to get right, the programmers who use your API will be happier. By focusing on usability, you show your respect for the happiness of the people who run your code.

That's why I care deeply about usability, and you should, too.

Shockingly Selective Bibliography

One of the things that continuously surprises me is just how few resources about user interface design are out there. Rather than include a huge bibliography that you may ignore, I've decided to include just six books, because I actually think you should go out and buy all of them. They are all that good.

Krug, Steve. *Don't Make Me Think*. Simon & Schuster Trade, 2000.

Laurel, Brenda (editor). *The Art of Human-Computer Interface Design*. Addison-Wesley, 1990.

Nielsen, Jakob. *Designing Web Usability: The Practice of Simplicity*. New Riders Publishing, 1999.

Norman, Donald. *The Design of Everyday Things*. Doubleday, 1990.

Tognazzini, Bruce. *Tog on Interface*. Addison-Wesley, 1992.

Tufte, Edward R. *The Visual Display of Quantitative Information*. Graphics Press, 1992.

BIBLIOGRAPHY

There are also a few Web sites worth visiting regularly:

- `useit.com`: Jakob Nielsen's Web site on usability

- `asktog.com`: Bruce Tognazzini's Web site on usability

- `joel.editthispage.com`: (Joel on Software), my own Web site

Index